The
Green Guide

FLORIDA

The Green Guide

Florida

A Travel Guide to Natural Wonders

Marty Klinkenberg and Elizabeth Leach
Illustrated by Dawn L. Nelson

Country Roads Press

CASTINE • MAINE

Green Guide to Florida
© 1993 by Marty Klinkenberg and Elizabeth Leach.
All rights reserved.

Published by Country Roads Press
P.O. Box 286, Lower Main Street
Castine, Maine 04421

Text and cover design by Studio 3, Ellsworth, Maine.
Illustrations by Dawn L. Nelson.

Library of Congress Catalog Card No. 93-070211.

ISBN 1-56626-025-6

Printed in the United States of America.
10 9 8 7 6 5 4 3 2 1

*We dedicate this book to
Ernie Klinkenberg,
who, despite his best efforts,
made camping fun and
nurtured respect for nature.*

Alabama

Georgia

1

Tallahassee

2

Orlando

3

Atlantic Ocean

5

4

Contents

Introduction

We were driving across the southern tip of Florida on Alligator Alley, a roadway that cuts through the Everglades from Fort Lauderdale to Naples.

Wading birds lined the canal on the north side and in all directions all one could see is the seemingly infinite River of Grass. Sawgrass waved like wheat in the wind and the horizon was as flat as a Kansas prairie.

At 55 miles per hour, the landscape is pleasant but difficult to appreciate. So we stopped and climbed from the car to stretch our legs – and to see if there really were alligators on Alligator Alley. We walked as near to the water as we could, but were disappointed to find our path impeded – and view interrupted – by a fence.

In a few minutes, we found ourselves atop a bridge and there we stood and stared. We saw cormorants and gallinules and turtles – and lots of lily pads – but no alligators. Slowly, as our eyes adjusted to the surroundings, alligators that had been there all along became apparent one by one.

Such is the beauty of natural Florida. There is far more to it than initially greets the eye. But taking the time to explore exposes one to a vast and delicate environment full of species threatened and endangered by the carelessness of man. The Florida panther, West Indian manatee, and Key deer of today are destined to be the dinosaurs of tomorrow if their suffering is ignored.

In touring Florida, we discovered the importance of being good environmental stewards. With only a few exceptions, the people we met were eager to educate and dedicated to conservation. Our thanks to them and to Don and Cathy Dunlap, who were our hosts on many research missions and contributed to the Green Guide.

To help clarify road designations, we used the following abbreviations: I = interstate, US = U.S. route or highway, and State = state route or highway.

1
The Florida Panhandle

APALACHICOLA NATIONAL
ESTUARINE RESEARCH RESERVE

It is easy to grasp the importance of the Apalachicola National
Estuarine Research Reserve. At 193,758 acres, it is the largest of
twenty-one federally monitored research estuaries, a list that
includes the Chesapeake and Narragansett bays and the Hudson
River.

The reserve, which includes the lower twenty miles of the
Apalachicola River, Apalachicola Bay, and St. George Island
State Park, is home to many plants and animals found nowhere
else in the world. The area has the greatest diversity of amphibians and reptiles in the United States and Canada and boasts
1,300 species of plants, 300 species of birds, 180 species of fish,
and 50 different mammals.

To get an appreciation for the ecosystem, which is threatened by tainted water flowing south from Atlanta, Georgia, visit
the reserve headquarters and tour free exhibits opened in 1992.
Displays cover a range of habitats found within the reserve and
contain some of the creatures that inhabit them. Exhibits include
a reptile display, an ocean reef aquarium, and tanks that simulate freshwater, saltwater, and brackish environments. Adjacent

1

aquariums imitate freshwater and saltwater marshes. A ten-station quiz is designed to teach you about the area. A caged area just inside the front door holds an alligator, a ball python, a broad-banded water snake, a corn snake, an eastern king snake, a gray rat snake, a Gulf Coast box turtle, and a pine snake.

A suwanee cooter was basking on a piece of driftwood next to a yellow-bellied slider when I viewed the 1,500-gallon tank that simulates the habitat of the Apalachicola River. Other amphibians include the unusual Barbour's map turtle, common snapping turtle, and eastern mud turtle. The American eel, black crappie, bluegill, bowfin, Florida gar, largemouth bass, and sunfish are among the freshwater fish found here.

The 1,500-gallon Apalachicola Bay tank, which simulates a brackish environment, contains an equally impressive collection of species, including the ornate diamondback terrapin, a speckled turtle indigenous only to the Apalachicola marine reserve. Also on display are tripletails (an unusual game fish), redfish, sheepsheads, and spotted sea trout.

The largest tank in the screened-in building is the 2,500-gallon Gulf of Mexico exhibit. Gag, red and scamp groupers, black and rock sea bass, mangrove and vermilion snappers, an ocellated moray eel, and pigfish live here.

Smaller aquariums that complement the larger tanks contain blue crabs, stone crabs, clams, and oysters, all of which are important to the region's commercial fishing–driven economy. Approximately 90 percent of the oysters harvested in Florida come from Apalachicola Bay, and 60 percent of the local citizens make their living from fishing.

The reserve is managed so as not to exclude traditional uses of natural resources. Hunting and sportfishing, as well as boating, camping, hiking, swimming, and commercial fishing, are allowed in most areas.

The chief purposes of the reserve are education and

research. The former is well served by the Estuarine Walk. The latter takes place in a laboratory on the premises.

Where: The reserve is located approximately ninety miles southwest of Tallahassee and sixty miles southeast of Panama City. Its headquarters is at 261 Seventh Street in Apalachicola.

Hours: The Estuarine Walk is open from 8:00 A.M. to 5:00 P.M. weekdays and from 10:00 A.M. to 3:00 P.M. some weekends. Call before a weekend visit.

Admission: Free.

Best time to visit: Anytime.

Activities: Examine exhibits of reptiles and freshwater and saltwater fish at the Estuarine Walk, adjacent to the office in Apalachicola. Bird watching and interpretive trips and hikes to bays, rivers, and barrier islands can be arranged by appointment.

Concessions: None.

Pets: Allowed in portions of the preserve but not in the exhibit area in Apalachicola.

Other: On-site educational opportunities include an audiovisual lending library, slide and audiovisual presentations, a guest lecture series, and teacher workshops. Brochures about the reserve also are available.

For more information:

Apalachicola National Estuarine Research Reserve, 261 Seventh Street, Apalachicola, FL 32320. 904-653-8063.

APALACHICOLA NATIONAL FOREST

The largest of Florida's national forests (600,000 acres), Apalachicola contains areas of ecological, geological, scenic, botanical, and recreational interest. It is far less developed than Ocala National Forest but not quite as primitive as Osceola.

A toothy alligator grin

More than 300 species of amphibians, birds, mammals, and reptiles live within the forest, which is fed by six rivers and streams. The topography includes lakes; lowlands covered by cypresses, oaks, and magnolias; remote swamps, sandhills, and flatwoods with stands of slash and longleaf pine; and wet, grassy savannas.

Detailed forest maps, available at the Wakulla District Ranger Station in Crawfordville, are of vital importance to anyone who wants to explore. This is a massive place with much to see and do, but one enjoyable primarily to those who like to investigate on their own.

The first place I stopped was Leon Sinks, a geological area less than six miles north of the Wakulla District Ranger Station on US 319. Sinkholes and depressions, formed when groundwater dissolved the underlying limestone bedrock, are of interest here.

Three marked trails — ranging from one-half mile to more than three miles — lead into a lush forest where dogwoods and southern magnolias grow along the path. Ash, beech, hickory, maple, red and white oak, slash pine, and tupelo trees, as well as wire grass, also can be seen.

You walk on a carpet of leaves and pinecones, with the wind rustling through the tops of moss-covered sixty- to eighty-foot trees. Roots in the path form natural steps, and the footing gets slippery on occasion because of the silky leaves.

You'll pass a number of shallow surface depressions before arriving at Hammock Sink, a wet sinkhole surrounded by a boardwalk. Hammock Sink is part of an underwater cave system with limestone rooms large enough to contain a six-story building. Submerged cavities and tunnels, mapped by expert divers, extend 1,300 feet horizontally and more than 200 feet deep.

The water in the sink basin is crystal clear, and fallen trees can be seen resting on the bottom. The opening to the much deeper cave system is imperceptible, and swimming and diving are prohibited. The walls of the sinkhole are so steep that anyone diving or falling in would have a hard time getting out.

Hammock Sink prepares you for the awesome appearance of deep, dark Dismal Sink, a short walk down the trail. A boardwalk also overlooks Big Dismal, where you can hear water running but can't seem to find the source. The view from the observation platform is breathtaking, with more than seventy-five plants cascading down the sink's steep walls.

The trail continues through sandy fields, past several more dry sinks and a wet sink, and through a gum swamp before returning to the trailhead. I met only two couples during an otherwise solitary tour, and one gentleman, a Tallahassee resident, acknowledged that this was his first visit. The fellow was as fascinated as I and vowed to return many times.

Although I didn't see any animals, a brochure on the geological area says that red-shouldered hawks, Carolina chickadees, great-crested flycatchers, wild turkeys, yellow-billed cuckoos, black racers, gopher tortoises, skinks, and white-tailed deer occasionally visit the area.

Apalachicola National Forest provides shelter and sustenance for a remarkable array of creatures. A vertebrate list acquired from the forest supervisor's office in downtown Tallahassee includes 45 amphibians, 189 birds, 68 fish, 47 mammals, and 67 reptiles.

The protected species that inhabit the forest include the alligator, alligator snapping turtle, American kestrel, bald eagle, Barbour's map turtle, Gulf sturgeon, indigo snake, and West Indian manatee. The most celebrated of all inhabitants, however, is the endangered red-cockaded woodpecker. Apalachicola National Forest is home to the world's largest population of these woodpeckers, with 685 active colonies in the spring of 1993.

Once a common bird in mature pine forests of the South, the species's range and population has been severely reduced by habitat destruction. It is endangered because the ancient pine trees needed for nesting are being cleared and much of the pine forest that remains is unsuitable for its purposes. The red-cockaded woodpecker is the only bird that nests and roosts in living southern pines. Unlike other woodpeckers, which create cavities in a matter of weeks, the red-cockaded woodpecker takes months and even years. Many cavities started are never completed, and others are stolen by larger, more aggressive birds.

The woodpeckers, which live in family units of two to nine birds, are most active in early morning and at night. They feed on insects and insect larvae close to their cavities, from which streams of sticky resin flow. This resin repels predators such as rat and indigo snakes, which climb straight up towering trees to ravage nests.

People rarely see the woodpeckers themselves, although bird-watchers have a better chance of seeing one at Apalachicola than anywhere else. Trees with nests have painted bands around the trunk to increase the number of sightings.

Bird-watchers also come to Apalachicola to see Bachman's sparrows, which, like red-cockaded woodpeckers, gravitate to forests of longleaf pine. American swallow-tailed and Mississippi kites, graceful raptors that nest in hardwood forests, are common in the summer. And one nesting pair of eagles was observed in the north end of the forest in the spring of 1993.

Hunting is allowed in portions of the forest, with hunts managed and regulations set by the Florida Game and Fresh Water Fish Commission. White-tailed deer are the main attraction, although waterfowl and small game such as bobwhite quail, gray squirrels, mourning doves, and rabbits also are hunted.

Good fishing opportunities abound throughout the forest. Anglers frequent the Ochlockonee and Apalachicola rivers and their many tributaries, as well as creeks, lakes, and streams. Fishing also is monitored by the game commission. A license is required of all fishermen, except children under fifteen and Florida residents age sixty-five or older. Nonresidents can purchase five-day or fourteen-day licenses at a tax assessor's office or some bait and tackle stores.

The forest is home to hundreds of plant species, many of which are threatened or endangered. A list provided by the forest supervisor's office lists three dozen sensitive species. Harper's beauty, an endangered species, was discovered in Apalachicola in 1963. It blooms during May along the side of Forest Road 180 and County 379 in the southwest region of the national forest.

Popular recreational activities include canoeing on the many creeks, lakes, and rivers and hiking the Apalachicola Trail, which covers approximately sixty miles, from US 319 on the east to the northwest corner of the forest at County 12.

Trout Pond, nine miles south of Tallahassee on County 373, was one of the first recreation areas developed exclusively for the physically challenged. Facilities, dedicated in 1970 by Mr. and Mrs. Dwight D. Eisenhower, Jr., include a specially designed swimming pool and partially covered fishing pier with safety rails, chair stops, and benches. Parking areas, rest rooms, drinking fountains, and picnic tables are modified to serve those who have difficulty using standard installations.

The paved, 700-foot Discovery Trail includes five educational stations that encourage learning about the environment through the senses. Benches and grassy areas provide rest stops along the trail, which has signs with oversize letters and a white line painted down the center to assist the visually impaired.

Trout Pond is open strictly for day use from April 1 through October 31, but it may be opened at other times upon request. Inquiries should be made at the Wakulla District Ranger Station in Crawfordville. Use is restricted to physically challenged visitors, their families and guests, senior citizens, and educational groups.

There are ten designated camping areas within the forest, but overnight tenting is not limited to them. Camping is permitted anywhere in the forest.

The most developed recreational facility is at Silver Lake, eight miles west of Tallahassee on County 260. Silver Lake offers a 250-foot white-sand beach, sixty-five picnic tables, forty-five campsites, and an interpretive trail.

Campsites are shaded and accommodate trailers up to twenty-two feet long. Each site has a concrete bench and grill or fire ring and is close to a rest room with a cold-water shower. No individual convenience hookups are available, but there is a central dumping station for trailers and faucets with potable water near most sites.

Picnic benches and pavilions allow a delightful view of the twenty-three-acre spring-fed lake, rimmed by large, moss-draped cypress and pine trees. The lake has a cordoned-off swimming area. No lifeguard is on duty, but a container with a life preserver is provided.

I visited a handful of camping areas in the forest, and my favorite by far was at peaceful and picturesque Wright Lake, off

Forest Road 101 a few miles from Sumatra. I drove through the campground at sunset and was overwhelmed by the aroma of campfires wafting through the air. The road within the campground is carpeted with pine needles, and the sites are spacious. The campground's volunteer hosts had planted beautiful flowers at the base of some pine trees and had constructed a birdhouse, both of which were nice touches.

Canoeing and fishing are permitted in the lake, which has a cordoned-off swimming area near the campground. I made several casts from shore at a disinterested largemouth bass that had taken up residence in the swimming area. A camper told me that fishermen catch bluegills and bass in deeper water at the edge of the swimming area.

Another campground is located at Hickory Landing, about one-half mile from Wright Lake on Forest Road 101B. The ten sites have picnic benches and fire rings and are convenient to drinking water and rest rooms. Stands of cypress grow along the shore and at the edge of a boat ramp on Owl Creek, which empties into the mighty Apalachicola River a few miles away. The creek was nearly at flood level when I visited in April, and fishing was slow due to the high water level. Angling improves in May and June when the water recedes. Largemouth bass and bluegills frequent the water around stumps and trees. Fishermen use crawfish to attract the large channel catfish on the bottom of the creek.

Only one of the five sites was being used when I visited the primitive campground at Wood Lake. This campground, popular with hunters, has concrete tables, fire rings, and drinking water. Chemical toilets, but no showers, are provided. A boat ramp allows fishermen access to bass and bluegills in the lake, which is a tributary of the Ochlockonee River.

The Munson Hills Off-Road Bicycle Trail offers a challenging ride through a towering longleaf pine forest and rolling sand dunes. The 7.5-mile loop trail dips into hammocks shaded by cherry, oak, and sassafras trees and provides many opportunities for viewing wildlife. Red-cockaded woodpeckers forage in trees along the trail, and threatened gopher tortoises burrow beside it. The trail starts approximately 1.25 miles south of the Tallahassee–St. Marks Historic Railroad State Trail at the parking lot on State 363.

Horseback riding is encouraged on all forest service roads, as well as on the Vinzant Riding Trail. The latter is a well-marked network of three trails traversing open pine forests and wetlands studded with wildflowers. Trails, open to the public for free, vary from ten miles round-trip to twelve miles one way. The trailhead is on Forest Road 342, not far from where it intersects State 267.

Where: The Wakulla District Ranger Station is located in Crawfordville, about eighteen miles south of Tallahassee on US 319. The Apalachicola District Ranger Station is located on State 20 in Bristol. Cities and towns that border the forest include Tallahassee, Crawfordville, Medart, Sopchoppy, Panacea, Hosford, and Bristol.

Hours: The Wakulla District Ranger Station is open from 7:30 A.M. to 5:00 P.M. Monday through Thursday and 7:30 A.M. to 4:00 P.M. Friday. The Apalachicola District Ranger Office is open from 7:30 A.M. to 5:00 P.M. Monday through Friday.

Admission: The only fee areas within the forest are at the Lost Lake and Silver Lake recreation areas. A day-use fee of $1.00 per vehicle is charged at Lost Lake, which offers swimming and picnicking. At Silver Lake, $2.00 per vehicle is charged to swim or picnic, and $5.00 per night is charged to camp.

Best time to visit: March and April. The weather is cool, bugs are minimal, and wildflowers are in bloom.

Activities: Bicycling, bird watching, camping, canoeing, fishing, hiking, horseback riding, hunting, and picnicking. No regularly scheduled ranger programs are offered.

Concessions: None.

Pets: Allowed in campgrounds and on trails provided they are leashed and under control. Owners should always be alert for alligators – which eat dogs – when near the water. No animals other than guide dogs are allowed in swimming areas.

Other: Field guides, maps, and other literature are available at the Apalachicola District and the Wakulla District Ranger Station.

For more information:

Wakulla District Ranger Station, U.S. Forest Service, Route 6, Box 7860, Crawfordville, FL 32327. 904-926-3561.

APALACHICOLA BLUFFS AND RAVINES PRESERVE

The Apalachicola Bluffs and Ravines Preserve contains eight natural and two man-made communities including sandhill, upland mixed forest, bluff, slope forest, bayhead and shallow drainages, seepage stream, floodplain forest, floodplain swamp, reservoir, and lawn.

The two dominant communities are the slope forest and the upland sandhill. The preserve contains a large number of remarkable ravines – extraordinary for a state that is so flat. The Apalachicola River has cut a swath through the countryside down past the water table, allowing springs to create ravine "fingers" to the side of the river. The slope forest grows along these banks and is very rare in the Southeast. The habitat contains a number of rare and endangered vegetation so hiking off the paths and on the slopes is prohibited.

The upland sandy communities suffered an aggressive logging program before The Nature Conservancy purchased the property in the mid-1980s. The Nature Conservancy is working to restore the longleaf pine and wiregrass community and to protect many of the endangered plant and animal species found here.

See the park by hiking the 3.5-mile loop trail. The hike is fairly strenuous due to the many different elevations, and in several areas only log bridges provide access across streams and shallow ravines. The self-guided trail leads you through upland and floodplain habitats to an overlook at Alum Bluff, so named for its white, chalky cliffs. Alum Bluff reveals three distinct geoogical ages and dates back to the Miocene period, roughly eighteen million years ago. An overlook at Alum Bluff is a beautiful spot to see the Apalachicola River, more than 180 feet below.

Guided tours are available for groups of ten people or more with advanced notice. To arrange for a tour, contact the preserve or The Nature Conservancy Headquarters in Winter Park at 407-628-5887.

Where: Located approximately four miles north of Bristol on County 12. Watch for the small hand-painted sign at the entrance.
Hours: Sunrise to sunset daily.
Admission: Free. A contribution to The Nature Conservancy is always cheerfully accepted.
Best time to visit: Spring, fall, and winter. Summer is hot and buggy.
Activities: Hiking. Bridges and log walkways permit passage over streams and rivulets.
Concessions: None.
Other: When visiting any nature conservancy preserve, pets, smoking, radios, camping, firearms, and off-road vehicles are prohibited. Spectacular flora blooms September to early November. Wearing bug repellent is highly advised.
Pets: Not permitted.
For more information:
Write The Nature Conservancy, Northwest Florida Land Steward, 625 North Adams Street, Tallahassee, FL 32301 or call 904-222-0199.

BLACKWATER RIVER STATE FOREST

Blackwater River State Forest is the best-kept secret in the state. I love it for all the reasons I don't care much for Ocala. In comparison, the development here is minimal, the forest is lush and green, and visitors are few. Still, there is much to do, and the surroundings are wonderful.

The 183,000-acre forest contains one of the country's finest remaining stands of longleaf pines and supports a variety of other vegetation. Clear-cutting is prohibited with only a few exceptions, so the landscape appears relatively untouched. Recreational opportunities abound, but you'll come away with the feeling that this is the way nature was meant to be.

At Blackwater River State Forest, you are largely left alone to explore. The forest is big enough to accept many visitors without seeming crowded, yet it is still largely ignored by all but residents of northwest Florida and southern Alabama.

The forest has so much to offer that it seems possible to do something different almost every day of the year. It has cold, clear spring-fed creeks for swimming and natural rivers for canoeing; lakes teeming with bass, bluegills, and catfish; designated trails for horseback riding; a twenty-one-mile system of hiking trails; campgrounds (with hot showers) overlooking picturesque lakes; places to picnic; and areas set aside for field-testing hunting dogs. Hunting is allowed during seasons managed by the Florida Game and Fresh Water Fish Commission.

The forest's wildlife is diverse and mostly nonthreatening. The birds include endangered red-cockaded woodpeckers, which live in the cavities of ancient longleaf pines, turkeys, and quail. Trees containing active woodpecker nests are banded to help visitors see one. Mammals include armadillos, bears, deer, hogs, opossums, rabbits, raccoons, red and gray foxes, skunks, and squirrels.

The two most popular areas within the forest are Krul and Bear lakes. Both are only a short drive from the twenty-four-hour Blackwater Forestry Center, where you can pick up free brochures and other visitor information.

The turnoff for the Krul Recreation Area is on State 4 East, directly across from the Munson Assembly of God Church. The road leading down to the six-acre lake is shaded by towering pines and dogwoods that bloom in the spring.

Spring-fed Krul Lake is restricted to swimming and is probably the busiest day-use area in the forest. The water is clear and inviting, if a bit cold. A boardwalk with ladders and platforms leads across the lake, providing access to the water at many spots.

Schools of plump bluegills and largemouth bass will follow you as you walk across the boardwalk. When I tossed some bread to them, the lake's surface turned into a boiling froth.

A wonderful picnic area with benches and grills slopes down to the lake. Sites in the nearby campground have tables, fire rings, water, and electricity. A daily fee must be left at a self-service pay station.

The 4.5-mile Sweetwater Hiking Trail starts 300 yards past the Krul Lake campground. It leads hikers over a swinging bridge that spans Sweetwater Creek and across Bear Lake Dam before intersecting the Jackson Trail. The latter is a 21-mile marked trail that is broken down into segments as short as three-quarters of a mile. The path, used by General Andrew Jackson during his historic 1818 journey to the Florida Territory, is now part of the Florida National Scenic Trail.

Fishing is excellent in 107-acre Bear Lake, created in 1959 by the Florida Game and Fresh Water Fish Commission. Sport fish include largemouth bass, sunshine bass, bluegills, shell-crackers, warmouths, and channel catfish. One angler I talked to reported having caught forty-one bass the previous day while using live threadfin for bait.

The lake has two boat ramps, a fishing pier accessible to people with disabilities, and a large area for bank fishing. No boat rentals are available, but bait and supplies can be procured in nearby Munson and Milton.

The campground at Bear Lake, less than a mile from the Krul Recreation Area, charges $8.00 for nonelectric sites and $10.00 for electric sites. Some sites overlook the lake, and others are shaded by pine trees.

Fishing is allowed in three other lakes, three major creeks, and numerous small streams within the forest. Other developed campsites that have no fees are at Hurricane and Karick lakes.

Coldwater Horse Trail has stables for 72 horses and kennels for 124 dogs. Many major bird-dog field trials have been held here since the facility opened in 1970, and hundreds of horseback riders use the trails each year. The trails take riders through forests of oaks, fragrant junipers, and soaring longleaf pines.

The Blackwater River, Sweetwater and Juniper creeks, and East Coldwater Creek offer excellent canoeing. Some of the canoe trails take more than a day to complete depending on water conditions and flow. No canoe rentals are offered within the forest, but a number of outfitters and rental agencies are located in the surrounding area.

Where: The forest headquarters/visitors center is near the intersection of State 4 and County 191 at Munson, seventeen miles northeast of Milton.

Hours: Day-use facilities are open from 7:00 A.M. to sunset. Campgrounds where fees are charged are open only to registered campers after dark.

Admission: A day-use fee of $1.00 per vehicle and fifty cents for each passenger other than the driver is charged at the Krul Recreation Area. Overnight campers pay $8.00, with an additional $2.00 assessed if electricity is used. Seniors pay $4.00 to camp plus $2.00 for electricity. The walk-in charge is fifty cents. The same camping fees are charged at the camping area at Bear Lake. Camping in other areas is free.

Best time to visit: Anytime is usually good, although bugs can be a problem in summer. It can get downright cold, with occasional snow, in winter.

Activities: Ranger-led group tours can be arranged through a forestry division supervisor. Bird watching, camping, canoeing, fishing, hiking, horseback riding, hunting, and swimming are popular within the forest.

Concessions: None, but outfitters in the area offer canoe rentals.

Pets: Allowed on a leash in primitive campgrounds, but not at Krul Lake, Bear Lake, Bone Creek, or Camp Paquette.

Other: Reservations are necessary for a designated campground for youth and church groups, kennels for dogs, stables for horses, and an educational center with dormitories and a dining hall.

For more information:

Blackwater River State Forest, 11650 Munson Highway, Milton, FL 32570. 904957-4201 or 957-4590.

BLACKWATER RIVER STATE PARK

The Blackwater River, one of the few remaining unspoiled rivers in Florida, runs fifty-eight miles southwest from its headwaters in Alabama's Conecuh National Forest before emptying into Blackwater Bay. The river's sandy bottom, tea-colored water, and pure white sandbars provide the backdrop for this 590-acre park along the southern border of Blackwater River State Forest.

The river, designated a Florida canoe trail, attracts visitors from all over the country. Its gentle current makes it ideal for beginning paddlers, and its wide, sandy banks and sandbars are perfect for picnicking, sunbathing, and swimming.

Not surprisingly, canoeing is the most popular form of

recreation here, and several outfitters in the area make things easy for you. Trips ranging from ninety minutes to three days can be arranged, with costs starting at $10.00 per person. Canoeing fees include all the necessary gear and a ride from the take-out area to the launching site. When you're done, you can simply beach your canoe at the take-out area and drive away. Single-person kayaks ($16.00), inner tubes ($6.00), and paddleboats ($12.00) also are available.

An eleven-mile canoe trip from Bryant Bridge to the take-out point within the park takes about four hours and is well worth the $11.00 investment. Tall cedars, magnolias, and longleaf pines grow along the river, and you can see the tracks of bobcats, turkeys, and white-tailed deer on the sandbars. Otters appear occasionally, and it's not unusual to see Mississippi kites soaring overhead in the summer.

Local outfitters include Andrew Jackson Canoes (904-623-4884), Blackwater River Canoe Rentals (904-623-0235), and Bob's Canoe Rentals and Sales (904-623-5457). Adventures Unlimited (904-623-6197 or 626-1699) also offers cabins, camp-sites, a catering service, and a wilderness store.

Two designated hiking areas are located within the 590-acre park – the ninety-minute Chain of Lakes Nature Trail and the sixty-minute Blackwater River Trail. The former begins at Deaton Bridge just inside the park entrance; the latter starts at a thirty-site campground.

The narrow, rugged Chain of Lakes Nature Trail runs along the edge of the river and leads through a swamp, past lakes, and into forests of longleaf pines and turkey oaks. Before embarking on your hike, walk out onto the bridge to take in a view of the river. The contrast between the dark water and the sandy bottom is astounding.

The path is steep in a few places, and it was so slippery when I visited the park in the spring that I had to turn back at the midway point. On my return, I found a dead snake in the middle of the trail. The eighteen-inch reptile had been killed minutes earlier by a hawk or an owl. The predator had fled at my approach but was sure to come back to feast on its victim.

The Chain of Lakes trail provides access to several natural beaches within a few minutes of a parking lot with a self-service pay station. Only a few people were taking advantage of the beaches when I was there.

The Blackwater River Trail, which starts at the campground, has white cedars growing along it edge. Be careful as you walk along the water because I was almost swallowed up by a patch of soft sand.

Several excellent interpretive signs detailing distinctive features of the river basin and the animals that inhabit it are located throughout the campground. Barred owls, opossums, rabbits, raccoons, red foxes, and skunks all live here. Bald cypress, red maple, and sweet bay trees are among the plant species found.

At the park's picnic area, boardwalks lead to five pavilions, bathhouses, and a swimming area along the river's edge. It seems quite wild and far removed from the parking area, even though it is only a short walk away. The water is clear in the shallow swimming area, where the current creates ripples in the submerged sand.

Where: Twelve miles northeast of Milton off US 90.

Hours: 8:00 A.M. to sunset. Only campers are allowed inside after sunset.

Admission: The fee for day use is $2.00 per vehicle for up to eight people. Camping is $8.00 for a site without electricity and $10.00 for a site with a hookup. Senior citizens pay half the camping fee.

Best time to visit: Labor Day through November.

Activities: Canoeing, fishing, hiking, picnicking, and swimming. No ranger-led activities are offered.

Concessions: None within the park, but several outfitters in the immediate area offer canoes, kayaks, paddleboats, and tubes.

Pets: Not allowed in camping or swimming areas. Guide dogs are always welcome.

Other: A list of birds, mammals, reptiles, and amphibians can be obtained from a ranger at the park entrance. Milton, about fifteen minutes away, is the seat of Santa Rosa County. Accommodations, department stores, groceries, and restaurants are located there.

For more information:

Blackwater River State Park, Route 1, Box 57-C, Holt, FL 32564. 904-623-2363.

PINE LOG STATE FOREST

This is the way camping was meant to be. My tent is pitched on a little knoll overlooking a picturesque lake. I am alone, with the exception of a recreational vehicle parked so far away I can hardly see it. Two hawks are circling overhead, and bluegills are biting my fishing line as soon as it hits the water. I'm fishing from the bank three steps behind my picnic bench, and the aroma of chicken barbecuing on my grill fills the air. In my opinion, this is heaven.

The campground, operated by the State Division of Forestry, is so wonderful and such a well-kept secret that it almost seems a sacrilege to tell anyone about it. But I will, grudgingly, out of a sense of duty.

Pine Log, one of Florida's first state forests, had nearly been stripped of trees when it was purchased in 1936. Now its 6,911 acres are covered with slash, sand and longleaf pines, and a variety of other trees.

The scenery here — a campground and picnic area between two beautiful lakes — is breathtaking. Cypress trees grow along the shore of the larger lake on the west side of the road. Pine trees rim the smaller lake to the east. The ground is lushly carpeted with soft pine needles.

Though small, the picnic area is among the most handsome I've seen. Benches and grills are situated in the midst of towering pines, and both lakes are visible from here. The picnic area also has a huge pavilion with a stone fireplace and six well-spaced tables. A sign advises that the pavilion is available by reservation only, but the ranger-in-residence invited me to use it. When I got there, logs were already burning in the fireplace.

The campground is well manicured, and most of its twenty sites are directly on the east lake. Those that aren't are nestled in the trees. Each site has a bench, grill, and water, and all but one have electrical hookups. A dumping station is available for recreational vehicles.

Both the east and west lakes are open for fishing and seem to be stocked with a good number of bluegills. I'm told large-mouth bass and catfish also are common. Small boats that are portageable can be used in both lakes, provided they are equipped only with electric motors. The east lake is small enough that a rowboat is sufficient, and the bluegill population is substantial enough to make it an ideal place for flycasting. The west lake has a boat ramp amid cypress trees. Swimming is allowed only in the east lake, but there is no lifeguard, the water is deep, and you must watch out for underwater obstructions.

The forest has four designated hiking trails, including an eight-mile portion of the Florida National Scenic Trail that passes through the campground and four lakes. The four-mile Dutch Tiemann Trail runs along Pine Log Creek.

You are likely to see small game and deer on any of the trails. I saw gray squirrels and a large, friendly fox squirrel in the campground. I also saw a great egret and little blue heron at the edge of the lake and constantly heard the hammering of woodpeckers. In the morning, I awoke to the crowing of roosters.

The Point Washington Wildlife Management Area crosses the forest boundaries, and hunting is permitted during scheduled seasons managed by the Florida Game and Fresh Water Fish Commission. Deer, which are plentiful, are the primary quarry. Dates and regulations are set by the commission, and no hunting is allowed in the vicinity of the campground.

The campground is plagued by several annoyances. The bathroom and showers are not convenient to a few campsites, and light poles are located at several spots around the east lake. I picked out what I thought was the best site in the campground, only to discover later that night that it was directly beneath a light. It was so bright that I could almost read inside my tent, although sites next to mine remained fairly dark.

One other disconcerting thing is that the campground is within a mile of a greyhound track in Ebro. The track announcer can be heard calling the races at night, which puts a damper on the wilderness experience.

Where: About fifteen miles north of Panama City Beach and one mile south of Ebro off State 79.

Hours: The picnic area and pavilion are open daily from 7:00 A.M. to sunset.

Admission: There is no charge for day use. Camping is $8.00 per night, $4.00 for senior citizens. Electricity is $2.00 extra. Group camping is $1.00 per person, with a minimum fee of $10.00.

Best time to visit: Hunting season, October to December, is busy. Camping sites are always available, although it's somewhat buggy in summer.

Activities: Camping, fishing, hiking, hunting, and swimming.

Concessions: None.

Pets: Allowed, but they must be leashed and are not permitted in buildings or campground lakes.

Other: Brochures and trail maps can be found in a mailbox along the park road. Ebro has a well-stocked convenience store and bait and tackle shop. There is no pay telephone in the park.

Contact the ranger-in-residence, who lives across the lake from the campground, in case of emergency.

For more information:

State Division of Forestry, 715 West Fifteenth Street, Panama City, FL 32401. 904-872-4175.

ST. GEORGE ISLAND STATE PARK

Nine miles of undeveloped beaches and sand dunes, surrounded by the Gulf of Mexico and Apalachicola Bay, provide the perfect

Planning a raid on your campsite

setting for this 1,848-acre park at the end of a long, narrow barrier island.

The dunes you see here are second in size only to those at St. Joseph Peninsula State Park, but they stand out just as much because of the coastal development that stops just short of the park gate. When you look out on the dunes, miles and miles of pure white beaches, forests of slash pines, and hammocks of oaks it is hard to believe that cattle were once raised here, troops used the island for training exercises in World War II, and target bombing was practiced on this very site.

The park, which was not opened for public use until 1980, is among the most popular in the region. Much of that has to do with the gorgeous beaches, nearly deserted when I stopped by on a cool spring day. The park is much busier in the warm summer months, but it can be appreciated at any time of the year.

St. George Island is a bird-watcher's paradise, particularly in the spring and fall. The island sits in the middle of the East Coast flyway, and 241 bird species have been recorded here. The route is used by peregrine falcons, which show up each October. Bald eagles nest within park boundaries in the spring. I saw a mother eagle with a chick sitting in their nest when I visited in early April. Ospreys, which begin nesting shortly after the eagles, had twenty active nests at the time. Some were visible in pine trees along the East Slough hiking trail. A ranger reported seeing a great horned owl, a fierce predator with a wingspan of nearly five feet, on the trail earlier that same week.

Other birds of interest include migrating warblers, which funnel through St. George Island in March, April, and May, the endangered snowy plover, and the American oystercatcher. The latter two species have declined because they nest directly on the beach and have lost much of their nesting grounds due to coastal development.

The island attracts the largest number of nesting loggerhead turtles in the northern Gulf of Mexico, with fifty-two nests dug in 1992. More than one hundred female turtles crawled ashore, but almost half were frightened away before nesting. Some were disturbed by lights; others fled due to the presence of coyotes, ghost crabs, and raccoons, all of which eat their babies or eggs.

Because the conditions are arid and the island is surrounded by water, the mammals that reside here are few. Gray squirrels and raccoons are common, and cottontail rabbits and river otters are seen occasionally near the saw grass marsh on the East Slough trail. A beaver, apparently flushed out of the flooded Apalachicola River, swam several miles across Apalachicola Bay and walked up the beach and into the park in early 1993.

The park has a transient alligator population, which also traverses the bay, and is home to the ornate diamondback terrapin. Water moccasins, the only poisonous snake in the park other than the diamondback rattlesnake, live in the saw grass marsh off the East Slough trail.

East Slough, which begins at the rear of the campground, is one of a few designated hiking areas within the park. The sandy trail is two miles one way and takes you through pine scrub, oak, and saw grass marshes. I saw no wildlife along this path, but blooming wildflowers make it lovely.

Several shorter trails follow boardwalks along the beach between the front gate and Sugar Hill, an area with high sand dunes five miles into the park. Interpretive signs explain the fragile dune communities, which are shaped by persistent winds that continually blow sand from one place to another. The boardwalk at Sugar Hill, which overlooks two-story dunes, had fallen victim to the process when I visited. A portion of it was buried under sand.

Surf and bay fishing can be good in the warmer months, with cobias, pompano, and Spanish mackerel caught in the surf at the east end of the island. Whitings are plentiful throughout most of the year.

Camping is available in a sandy, open sixty-site area. Each site has a bench, grill, water, and access to electricity.

Bathhouses with hot showers are provided. Reservations are suggested, especially from March to Labor Day. Because the campground was full, campers were being turned away the day I visited in April.

Where: Across a causeway from US 98 at Eastpoint, a fishing village just east of Apalachicola.

Hours: The park is open from 8:00 A.M. to sunset for day use. Only campers are allowed in the park after dark.

Admission: $3.25 per vehicle for up to eight passengers. Additional passengers, bicyclists, and pedestrians are $1.00 each. Camping is $8.48 for sites with a bench, grill, and water. Sites with electricity are $10.60 per night.

Best time to visit: October and March through May.

Activities: Several special ranger-led programs are held during turtle-nesting season in July. Slide shows and talks are held during the summer. Call for details. Bird watching, fishing, sunbathing, and swimming are the most popular recreations.

Concessions: None.

Pets: Discouraged, with the exception of guide dogs. Pets are not allowed in the camping area, on the beach, in the water, or on trails.

Other: Park literature, including lists of birds, mammals, reptiles, amphibians, and shells, are available at the ranger station. The bugs can be terrible in the summer. Several convenience stores and restaurants are located on the island.

For more information:

St. George Island State Park, P.O. Box 62, Eastpoint, FL 32328. 904-927-2111.

OCHLOCKONEE RIVER STATE PARK

As campers stream from Florida to the Great Smoky Mountains in summer and from northern cities to more familiar Florida haunts in fall and winter, most bypass this little park. It's a shame, because this 392-acre parcel, which was previously part of St. Marks National Wildlife Refuge, offers perfect examples of the scenery along the Gulf Coast of North Florida and many recreational opportunities as well.

The picnic area alone makes a visit worthwhile. Several sites are directly on the Dead and Ochlockonee rivers, and some sites have ramps leading down to the water. Pavilions are available for large groups. Individual sites, most shaded by towering trees draped with Spanish moss, each have a table and an elevated grill, with trash containers and water faucets handy.

The park's designated swimming area is adjacent to the picnic grounds. The sandy beach faces the Dead River and is cordoned off. Though clean, the water is very dark and not particularly inviting. No lifeguard is on duty, and signs remind swimmers to be wary of alligators.

Fishing is permitted from the bank, and both freshwater and saltwater species inhabit the area. The park is approximately six miles inland from the Gulf of Mexico, and the water's salt content fluctuates during the year, providing an environment that can be acceptable at times for saltwater species. Largemouth bass, bream, catfish, speckled perch, butterfish, flounder, redfish, spotted sea trout, and, occasionally, even Spanish mackerel are caught. Freshwater and saltwater licenses are required. Bait is available in Sopchoppy.

The park has a boat ramp with a fish-cleaning station and convenient rest rooms. Those renting canoes set out from here to investigate the nearby creeks, where you may encounter endangered manatees and dolphins. The Ochlockonee River Lower Canoe Trail, which begins twelve miles west of Tallahassee at Lake Talquin, ends in the park. The canoe trail, almost entirely within Apalachicola National Forest, is relatively pristine and winds through a variety of habitats.

The campground has thirty sites for tents and recreation vehicles up to about twenty-five feet long, as well as a youth camping area that can accommodate one hundred people. The campground has rest rooms and hot showers and is the only place I have seen the white squirrel. This exotic animal, freed from a local collection, has begun to interbreed with the gray squirrel and shares many of the same behaviors. Florida black bears, bobcats, deer, foxes, fox squirrels, and gopher tortoises also live in the park.

Endangered red-cockaded woodpeckers may be observed in pine trees next to the pond along the park's scenic drive. Orange ribbons have been placed around the trunks of trees that contain woodpecker nests. Other birds commonly seen include bald eagles, blue herons, and ospreys.

Where: Four miles south of Sopchoppy on US 319.

Hours: 8:00 A.M. to sundown daily.

Admission: The day-use fees are $2.00 per vehicle and $1.00 for bicyclists and pedestrians. Campers pay $10.70 per night for sites without electricity and $12.84 per night for sites with electricity from March 1 through September 30. Sites are $2.00 less the rest of the year.

Best time to visit: The weather is most pleasant in October and November. The park is busiest from the middle of April through September. It was nearly empty – and wonderfully quiet – when I visited on April 1.

Activities: No ranger-led programs are offered, but you'll find more than enough to keep you busy. Choices include a seven-mile scenic drive, walks through a pine forest and along a river, boating, camping, canoeing, fishing, picnicking, swimming, and waterskiing.

Concessions: Canoes can be rented for $7.49 per half day or $10.70 per day.

Pets: Not allowed in the campground or swimming areas. They must be kept on a six-foot, hand-held leash and well behaved at all times.

Others: The campground and picnic area offer special play areas for children. The honor system is used for day use, with fees deposited in an envelope. Campers select their own sites. A ranger collects the fees at sundown.

For more information:

Ochlockonee River State Park, P.O. Box 5, Sopchoppy, FL 32358. 904-962-2771.

PONCE DE LEON STATE RECREATION AREA

Local residents flock to Ponce de Leon Springs in the summer to refresh themselves in the clear, 68°F water. Churches baptize their members in the swimming hole, and families use the tidy park for reunions.

The small spring is surrounded by a concrete wall and has a diving platform and two ladders leading into the water. Water gushes out of the spring at a rate of fourteen million gallons per day from a boil twenty-three feet below the surface. Largemouth bass and bluegills are easy to see as they rest against the sandy white bottom in the middle of the spring.

Two nature trails depart from the swimming area, both short enough to be negotiable for children. The Spring Run Trail is a tranquil twenty-minute walk through shady, moss-draped cypress trees. It runs along a dark, spring-fed creek studded with occasional sandbars. Sparkleberry and American holly are among the trees seen. The Sandy Creek Trail is a half-hour stroll along a clear stream. The footpath, a bit slippery when I visited in April, leads through cypress and southern magnolia trees. A turtle, startled by my presence, plopped noisily off a tree branch into the water as I walked past.

The park has a small picnic area shaded by oak trees. Wildflowers were blooming when I was there. Fishing is allowed everywhere except in the swimming area.

Vortex Springs, about five miles north of I-10 off State 81 on the outskirts of Ponce de Leon, is a developed diving resort that caters to cave divers. It has nature and horse trails and offers canoe, paddleboat, and tube rentals. Camping and picnic areas are located adjacent to the spring, along with a lodge with both private rooms and dormitory-style accommodations. Costs range from $14.00 per night for a campsite with electricity to $80.00 per night for a dormitory that holds twenty-six people.

Several dozen divers were in the water when I visited. The spring is shallow around the edge and plummets to a depth of 63 feet at the cave mouth. A sign posted at the cave entrance warns inexperienced or unqualified divers of the extreme danger. Where the cave slopes to a depth of 110 feet, access is restricted to experts.

A flood-control system keeps the spring crystal clear all the time, even when other springs in the vicinity are cloudy due to storm runoff. Divers can rest on underwater platforms, and handrails and arrows point the way inside the cave. Night diving is allowed and is part of a Monday through Thursday package that costs $15.00 per day, including one free air fill each day.

No fishing is allowed in the spring, but species include the three-foot grass carp, Japanese goldfish that weigh five to ten pounds, bass, bluegills, catfish, and eels. You can buy a package of fish food for twenty-five cents at the diving shop and feed the fish from docks extending into the spring. If you return the empty bag to the shop, you get your quarter back.

The daily flow of this spring is 25 million gallons, but it passes almost without notice because the area is so large. For information, contact Vortex Springs, Route 2, Box 650, Ponce de Leon, FL 32455, 904-836-4979 in Florida or 800-342-0640 elsewhere in the United States.

Morrison Springs, off County 181A about four miles south past Ponce de Leon Springs, is less developed. Swimming is $1.50, and tubes can be rented for $1.50. When I visited in

March, the spring was closed due to cloudy water. When the water is clear, it is open seven days a week, Monday through Thursday, 7:00 A.M. to 8:00 P.M.; and Friday through Sunday, 6:00 A.M. to 10:00 P.M. The facility includes a boat ramp, a small beach, an air station, showers, and refreshments. There is a diving fee of $10.00, and all divers must have a certification card. For information contact Morrison Springs, P.O. Box 95, Ponce de Leon, FL 32455, 904-836-4223.

Where: One-half mile south of US 90 on County 181A in Ponce de Leon.
Hours: 8:00 A.M. to sunset daily.
Admission: $2.00 per vehicle.
Best time to visit: Right after Labor Day. The park is busiest from June through Labor Day.
Activities: Swimming and picnicking. No ranger-led programs are offered.
Concessions: None.
Pets: Allowed on a leash on nature trails and in the picnic area. They are not permitted in the swimming area or the water.
Other: For safety reasons, scuba diving is not allowed in the spring, but it is permitted at private facilities in nearby Vortex Springs and Morrison Springs.
For more information:
    Ponce de Leon State Recreation Area, Route 2, Box 1528, Ponce de Leon, FL 32445. 904-836-4281.

ST. JOSEPH PENINSULA STATE PARK

I walked along the beach in St. Joseph park on a chilly, misty, unseasonable day in early April. But rather than ruin the experience, the conditions seemed to accentuate the beauty of this place. It was hard to believe I was in Florida and not on some deserted island off Cape Cod or the Canadian Maritimes.

More than 100,000 visitors come to St. Joseph each year, primarily during the best beach weather in the summer. But this weather was just fine for me. The peninsula's fourteen miles of white-sand beaches were deserted but for a handful of beachcombers reveling in the seclusion.

The beach and its enormous dunes are what make St. Joseph unique. A stroll along the beach, which is accessible by boardwalks leading from two campgrounds, takes you past dunes 60- to 80-feet high. The dunes form a natural barrier against storms and protect the shoreline from erosion, a fact that escaped the grasp of homeowners just outside the 2,516-acre park. Residents of the overly developed coastline are now complaining that their property is being periodically washed away.

Shorebirds paid scant attention to me as I strolled along the beach, occasionally stooping to examine shells. A black-necked stilt, a tall shorebird with a long beak, followed me step for step for a short distance. We walked to the accompaniment of the surf crashing over clear, shallow sandbars in the Gulf of Mexico.

St. Joseph is not always so serene, but it is always worth a visit. It is a reminder of the way the Florida coastline used to be and is large enough to offer some solitude even at its busiest.

More than 200 species of birds have been recorded here. The area is home to one of the country's most spectacular hawk migrations each fall, and it is the only place in northwest Florida where the endangered peregrine falcon may be seen with regularity.

Anyone planning a visit to the park in late September or October stands an excellent chance of seeing a large number of hawks. The first three or four days following a cold front are the best bird-watching days, with possibly 200 to 300 hawks observed. The record for one hour is 600, and more than 1,500 per day may be present if the conditions are perfect.

The most abundant hawk is the sharp-shinned. Others include the broad-winged, Cooper's, marsh, red-shouldered, and red-tailed hawks. Kestrels, merlins, Mississippi kites, ospreys, and peregrine falcons also frequent the area. The best place to observe birds is along the beach and bayshore. I saw hundreds of shorebirds and a little blue heron while walking on the beach between campgrounds.

Endangered sea turtles nest along the beaches from May to September. Seventy nests were counted in 1992, but half were destroyed by coyotes. Other mammals commonly seen are bobcats and deer.

The National Park Service has rated St. Joseph as having the best recreational potential of any area between Brownsville, Texas, and the Florida Keys. Unusual opportunities include crabbing, scalloping, scuba diving, shelling, and surfing.

The park has four places to camp: two developed facilities, a youth camping area with only toilets and cold showers, and primitive sites in a 1,700-plus-acre wilderness preserve at the north end of the peninsula. The two developed campgrounds offer 119 sites, 97 of which have access to electricity. All the sites have benches, grills, and water, and bathhouses with hot showers and rest rooms are conveniently located. A dump station is provided for recreational vehicles. Sites in Camping Area 1 are sparsely vegetated and not very shady. I prefer Camping Area 2, where sites are better shaded and seem less crowded because there are more trees.

The developed campgrounds are often full, and reservations are suggested. The staff will reserve up to half the sites on any given day and offer whatever else is available on a first-come, first-served basis. Be there early, or be prepared to be turned away.

Eight remote cabins, with names such as Porpoise, Snapper, and Starfish, are always occupied. The cabins have a stunning view of St. Joseph Bay, and each has a boardwalk leading to the water. They are completely furnished and have fireplaces and screened porches facing the bay. It's no wonder some people reserve them a year in advance. A minimum stay of five nights is required from March 1 to September 15 and two nights from September 16 to February 28. The cabins accommodate up to seven people. Deer and foxes sometimes are seen on the beach behind the cabins.

Hikers can camp almost anywhere in the wilderness preserve, which begins two miles past the developed campgrounds. The only access is by foot, and all supplies, including water, must be carried in and out. There are no facilities, not even outhouses. One veteran camper told me he often canoes along the beach to the wilderness area, which reduces the load considerably.

Campers should be aware of pesty raccoons, particularly in developed camping areas. At times, the problem is severe. The raccoons will rip through a tent's screen door if food is left inside, and they consider any window, open even a few inches, an invitation to pillage. Rangers report having to retrieve cameras, luggage, and purses pilfered by foraging raccoons.

The park boasts several hiking trails, including a thirty-minute walk just inside the entrance. This trail leads through longleaf and slash pines, oaks, firs, and magnolias to the shore of St. Joseph Bay. Another forty-five minute trail is adjacent to a picnic area on the side of the island opposite Camping Area 1. The trail passes through pine scrub and salt marsh and continues along the bayshore. Gray foxes, raccoons, and striped skunks are common here. A thirty-minute trail extends along the beach between the boardwalks leading from the developed camping areas.

Surf fishing is one of the most popular recreations here. The fishing is best when the weather begins to warm up in April and May. Species include bluefish, cobias, flounder, king mackerel, pompano, redfish, sea trout, sharks, sheepsheads, and whitings.

Where: Approximately twenty miles from Port St. Joe off County 30, west of US 98. From Port St. Joe, get on US 98 going east to County 30, take County 30 until you see signs directing you to Cape San Blas and St. Joseph Peninsula State Park. From Apalachicola, take US 98 west to County 30, follow it until you see a sign for Cape San Blas and St. Joseph Peninsula State Park.

Hours: The park is open for day use from 8:00 A.M. to sunset daily. Only campers are allowed in the park after dark.

Admission: Day use is $3.25 per vehicle containing up to eight people and $1.00 per person over eight. Bicyclists and pedestrians pay $1.00. Camping is $15.90 per night from March 1 to October 31 and $8.48 per night from November 1 to February 28. Senior citizens pay half. Electricity is an additional $2.12 per night. Walk-in campsites are $3.00 for adults and $2.00 for youths age eighteen and under.

Best time to visit: The park is busiest in the summer, even though it is often buggy and hot. The weather is most pleasant in the spring and fall.

Activities: No ranger-led activities are offered. Boating, camping, fishing, hiking, picnicking, and swimming are available.

Concessions: Cabins can be rented for $58.30 per night from September 16 to February 28 and $74.20 per night during the rest of the year. Rental bikes are $2.00 per hour or $10.00 per day. Canoes are $3.00 per hour or $15.00 per day, and a $20.00 deposit is required. A fee of $2.00 is charged to use the boat ramp at the park marina on St. Joseph Bay.

Pets: Not allowed on the Gulf beaches or in the park overnight. They are permitted on a leash in a designated picnic area and on a bay beach.

Other: Extensive literature on the park is available from a ranger upon checking in. A well-stocked convenience store and restaurants are handy to the park. A store at the marina carries fishing supplies and sundries but is open only during the summer.

For more information:
St. Joseph Peninsula State Park, Star Route 1, Box 200, Port St. Joe, FL 32456. 904-227-1327.

ST. MARKS NATIONAL WILDLIFE REFUGE

I had driven many hours to get to St. Marks, and my expectations were great upon arriving here. But even so, the refuge didn't disappoint me. This place is magnificent, from the exhibits in the visitors center to the view of Apalachee Bay at the end of the 6.8-mile Lighthouse Road.

One of the oldest federal wildlife refuges, St. Marks was created in 1931 to provide a wintering and resting area for migratory waterfowl. Today its 65,000 acres include a diversity of habitats that protect an amazing assortment of birds, amphibians, mammals, and reptiles.

The refuge's bird inventory lists 294 species, 94 known to nest within the boundaries. Its wetlands host thousands of migrating ducks from mid-November through late December, and shorebirds are common in the late spring and fall.

When I visited near the end of March, there were ten active eagle nests, and as many as thirteen or fourteen fledglings were expected to be produced. Endangered red-cockaded woodpeckers were expected to begin nesting the following month. Sightings reported on the day I was there included parula, pine, and prothonotary warblers; bald eagles; a red-breasted merganser; ospreys; green-winged teal; rail; ruby-throated hummingbirds; ruby-crowned kinglets; least bitterns; red-cockaded woodpeckers; and rufous-sided towhees.

The refuge is home to thirty-four confirmed amphibians, fifty-two reptiles, and fifty mammals. Some of the more unusual inhabitants include the two-toed amphiuma, eastern hognose snake, and jaguarundi. The amphiuma is a two-foot-long aquatic salamander that feeds on fish, snakes, and frogs. The hognose snake confuses enemies by hissing, inflating its body with air, and rolling around on the ground. And the jaguarundi, twice the

A male anhinga dries his wings

size of a domestic house cat, is rare north of Mexico but sighted often here. Repeat visitors also might see alligators, bobcats, deer, and river otters on the main road.

I began my visit by examining the extensive exhibits at the recently renovated visitors center. Displays depict and explain eight habitats found within the refuge and detail the animals and plants common to each. Dioramas show wintering waterfowl, red-cockaded woodpeckers, alligators, and otters.

The refuge offers many marvelous means of viewing wildlife, but I chose to do what most visitors do – drive the nearly seven-mile scenic Lighthouse Road. The road, which is really a continuation of County 59, is the principal access route into the refuge. It passes through pine flatwoods, hardwood swamps, managed freshwater ponds, and tidal salt marshes. Trails, observation platforms, interpretive displays, and picnic tables are available along the way. The road ends at the St. Marks Lighthouse, in operation since 1831.

The drive along Lighthouse Road turned out to be so fascinating that I often found myself stopping, backing up, crawling along, and, eventually, worrying about the time. I arrived at midafternoon and spent almost three hours on the drive alone. An excellent drive guide, available for under $1.00 at the visitors center, was a valuable tool.

The drive begins in a dense hardwood swamp with stumps submerged in the water along both sides. The guide says ospreys nest in the tall cypress trees, wood ducks nest in tree cavities, and warblers are plentiful in the spring and fall (although I saw none).

Nearby is a series of managed ponds, where I watched a great blue heron chase away a great egret and steal its perch atop lily pads. An anhinga was drying its wings a short distance away, and an endless stream of ducks flew overhead.

A few minutes later, I was stopped in my tracks and found myself driving in reverse when I came upon an osprey roosting on a bare branch several hundred yards across Mounds Pools. After a short time the bird took off, and I watched as it flew in slow deliberate circles as it searched for food.

Stopping to watch the osprey allowed me to see a number of other birds that had been difficult to spot as I was driving. While standing in just one spot, I saw mottled, ring-necked, and ruddy ducks; northern pintails; an American wigeon; a snowy egret; a great egret; a little blue heron; and common moorhens.

After continuing on for a short distance, I stopped to hike along the one-mile Mounds Nature Trail, so named because it crosses over an Indian mound. The refuge was occupied by Swift Creek Indians around 500 A.D. The trail cuts through pine flatwoods, an oak ridge, and an oak-and-cabbage-palm hammock and skirts a brackish pond and saltwater marsh. Although many bird-watchers enjoy this trail during the winter and spring, when the woods are said to be filled with small, migrating songbirds, I saw only wading birds, including little blue and tricolored herons.

I continued to the end of the drive at the lighthouse, which fronts Apalachee Bay and is bordered by Lighthouse Pool. Hundreds, perhaps thousands, of shorebirds took off with my intrusion. I walked along the Levee Trail, a half-mile round-trip that leads to a rock jetty, and wished I had brought along my fishing rod. The spot is popular with anglers, who fish for redfish, Spanish mackerel, and spotted sea trout.

I came across several groups of fishermen on Lighthouse Road, all pursuing panfish from the banks of freshwater impoundments. Fishing is always allowed, but the ponds are closed to boats and canoes from October 15 to March 15. A boat ramp is provided for saltwater fishermen in a protected area near the lighthouse.

The two short trails I walked are but the tip of the iceberg here. The refuge's network of trails attracts many hikers during the winter months, when temperatures are cooler and there are fewer bugs. The trails range in distance from the one-third-mile

Plum Orchard Pond Trail directly behind the visitors center to a nine-mile primitive trail in the nearby Panacea Unit. The thirty-five-mile portion of the Florida National Scenic Trail has trailheads in the adjacent Aucilla Wildlife Management Area and at Medart on US 98.

Hunting is allowed for resident game species in designated areas from fall through spring. Contact the refuge for dates, regulations, and permits. The hunts are supervised by the Florida Game and Fresh Water Fish Commission.

Picnic benches are available on the edge of a lake just off the main road next to Mounds Trail. Another picnic area is located at Otter Pond in the Panacea Unit.

For optimum pleasure, you should arrive early and stay late. I left fulfilled after a long afternoon, but I could have easily extended my visit to a full day or even two.

Where: The visitors center is on County 59, three miles south of US 98 at Newport.

Hours: The refuge office and visitors center are open from 8:00 A.M. to 4:15 P.M. Monday through Friday and 10:00 A.M. to 5:00 P.M. Saturday and Sunday. Both are closed on federal holidays. All facilities within the refuge, other than the boat ramp at Lighthouse Pool, close at sunset.

Admission: $3.00 per car, $15.00 for commercial vans or buses with twenty or fewer people, and $25.00 for vans and buses with more than twenty people.

Best time to visit: December through February.

Activities: Ranger- or volunteer-led programs, including bird and flower walks, are held year-round. Contact the visitors center for details. The Mounds Trail is a one-mile interpretive loop and just one of many hiking areas within the refuge. There are seventy-five miles of trails, including a thirty-five-mile section of the Florida National Scenic Trail. Bicycling is allowed on the trails and along the main park road.

Concessions: None.

Pets: Must be on a leash and under control at all times. Recently, a dog allowed to run loose while on a leash was eaten by an alligator at Lighthouse Pool.

Other: The displays at the visitors center offer a great introduction to the refuge. A wonderful selection of literature and gift items, including children's books and bluebird boxes, is available. Lists of amphibians, birds, mammals, plants, and reptiles also are available, along with activity schedules, descriptions of hiking trails, and maps. The refuge has no overnight accommodations or food service, but campgrounds, lodging, and restaurants are located throughout the surrounding area.

For more information:

St. Marks National Wildlife Refuge, P.O. Box 68, St. Marks, FL 32355. 904-9256121.

FLORIDA CAVERNS STATE PARK

As a Florida native and lifelong South Florida resident, I've grown accustomed to flat land with only minor topographical changes. Because of that, it is hard to imagine the rolling foothills, deep springs, and waterfalls of northwest Florida, much less the region's expansive caves.

I visited Florida Caverns State Park not expecting a lot. I had toured Mammoth Cave National Park in Kentucky several summers back and anticipated a much less dramatic and miniature version in my own state. I can't begin to tell you how wrong I was. Maybe it is simply unabashed allegiance, but I found Florida Caverns to be at least the equal of the much more famous national park.

Tours begin with a short orientation film in the visitors center. Take time to examine the exhibits there before watching the film because the two combined explain the region's geological and historical significance.

The tour itself is unhurried and fascinating. You walk amid astounding formations, created over thousands and tens of thousands of years, crouch to get through places where the ceiling is low, and even come face to face with bats.

I saw three bats during my visit, one so close that I was afraid to exhale lest I disturb it. The bat was clinging to the wall in a narrow, low-lying tunnel through which I had to stoop and walk sideways to pass. The experience made a few members of my group squeamish, but most, like me, found it more interesting than scary. The bat population has decreased considerably in recent years, so I felt blessed to have seen one. They are tiny, harmless creatures that fill a critical niche in nature as one of the most effective means of insect control.

Rooms visited during the tour have stalactites growing down from the ceiling and stalagmites growing up from the cave floor. Formations caused by acidic water seeping into limestone bear a remarkable resemblance to animals, corkscrews, drapes, fishhooks, flying buttresses, gabled windows, pipe organs, soda straws, waterfalls, and even a wedding cake.

We navigated through natural passages called Tall Man's Torment and Fat Man's Squeeze without a single fatality. At one point, we stood in inky darkness and contemplated how frightening and difficult it would be to find one's way without electricity, guide, or headlamp. We proceeded carefully because the floor is damp and slippery much of the way.

Visitors are asked not to touch formations because they are brittle and easily stained by human hands. But our tour guide took us to one spot where a column had been sacrificed to satisfy the curiosity of guests. The so-called touching post was cold and slick to the hand.

The cost of the tour — $4.00 — is minimal for the education and entertainment you receive. It was among the more pleasant surprises of my statewide tour.

What makes Florida Caverns all the more mysterious is that

new formations and caves are being discovered all the time. Twenty-three caves have been mapped in the park, and more than thirty other surface holes have been identified but are as yet unexplored. A cave almost as large as the one examined during the tour was discovered directly under the visitors center in 1980. Explorers found two spectacularly decorated rooms with ceilings sixteen feet high covered with undisturbed formations.

Although more than half of the 125,000 visitors annually come to Florida Caverns only to see the caves, there is more to the place than that. Camping is appealing in the park's quiet, thirty-two-site campground. Sites are spacious and fairly isolated, and each has a bench, a grill, water, and an electrical outlet. Rest rooms and showers are centrally located, and bundles of firewood are sold for $3.00 at the entrance station.

Swimming is popular in Blue Hole Spring, clear most of the year but cloudy during my visit in April. Diving in the spring is allowed but not recommended because conditions are less than ideal. The cave is silty and plummets to a depth of eighty-five feet, and diving is considered dangerous for all but the most experienced divers.

Fishing is permitted in the vicinity of the spring but is better farther down the Chipola River. A boat and canoe launch across from the campground provides easy access to the river. Bass, bluegills, catfish, and speckled perch are the most sought species. A freshwater license is required for everyone but youths under sixteen and senior citizens who are residents of Florida.

Two trails take horseback riders through upland and floodplain areas where deer, bobcats, otters, and turkeys are occasionally seen. The trails total more than seven miles. Markers are provided at each turn or junction. Facilities include a stable with covered stalls, a corral, a group-camping facility, individual primitive campsites, a picnic pavilion, rest rooms, and showers. Proof of a negative Coggins test is required.

Walkers can tour horse trails when they are not flooded.

They also can enjoy a system of short nature walks that start a short distance from the visitors center. Trails lead along limestone bluffs and drop to the floodplain swamp of the Chipola River. Several caves and some northern plant life can be seen during leisurely thirty-minute strolls on the Beech-Magnolia and Floodplain trails.

Where: Three miles north of Marianna on County 166.

Hours: 8:00 A.M. to sunset for day use. Only campers are allowed in the park after dark.

Admission: Day-use fees are $3.25 for a driver and vehicle carrying up to eight passengers. Bicyclists, extra passengers, members of organized groups, and pedestrians are $1.00 each. Campers pay $12.72 per night from March 1 to September 30 and $8.48 per night the rest of the year. Electricity is $2.12 per night extra. Horseback riders pay $5.00 for one rider and horse, $10.00 for two riders and two horses, $12.00 for three or four riders and three or four horses, and $17.00 for five riders and five horses.

Best time to visit: Camping is most pleasant in October, when the weather is mild. It can be cold and wet in winter, with temperatures at night dipping into the twenties or lower. Portions of the caverns may be flooded in January, February, and March, and tours are occasionally shortened because of it.

Activities: Guided cave tours are given twenty minutes apart from June through August and one hour apart during the rest of the year. Tours begin at 9:00 A.M. year-round, with the last at 3:45 P.M. in the winter and 5:00 P.M. in the summer. The cost is $4.00 for adults and $2.00 for children ages three to twelve. Fishing, hiking, and swimming are popular.

Concessions: Three-person canoes can be rented at the ranger station for $7.00 per half day and $10.00 per full day.

Pets: Not allowed on beaches or in buildings, the campground, caves, or swimming areas. They are permitted in picnic areas and on nature trails if they are on a six-foot, hand-held leash. Guide dogs are always welcome.

Other: An orientation film on the caverns is shown at the gift shop/visitors center, from which cave tours depart. Fine displays of artifacts, fossils, and other regional exhibits also are offered in the visitors center, which is open from 9:00 A.M. to 5:00 P.M. daily except Thanksgiving and Christmas.

For more information:

Florida Caverns State Park, 3345 Caverns Road, Marianna, FL 32446. 904-4829598.

2
North Florida

MARJORIE KINNAN RAWLINGS
STATE HISTORIC SITE

It was nearly dusk on a cool, breezy Saturday in the spring when I stepped through the rusty gate into Marjorie Kinnan Rawlings's backyard at Cross Creek. Here Rawlings wrote her 1939 Pulitzer Prize–winning novel *The Yearling*, the compelling story of a boy and his adopted fawn. The fragrant blossoms of oranges, grapefruits, and tangerines were almost overwhelming as I walked through the small citrus grove where Rawlings found peace and inspiration. She lived here off and on from 1928 until her death in 1953. During that period, she also wrote *Cross Creek, Golden Apples, Secret River,* and *The Sojourner.*

The property, listed on the National Register of Historic Sites since 1970, has been maintained to look as it did when Rawlings lived here. Eight acres are managed by the Florida Department of Natural Resources. The remaining sixty acres are controlled by Alachua County Parks and the University of Florida Foundation.

It is easy to see why Rawlings felt an immediate affinity for this place. The house was closed when I visited, but as I walked the grounds, I felt as though I'd stepped back in time.

45

My imagination went into overdrive as I strolled through the garden the author had tended four decades earlier and peered through the windows of the Oldsmobile bearing a 1940 license plate parked in her driveway. In the chicken coop, a baby chick sat in the middle of its mother's back, and other chicks peered out from beneath her wings. A cat stared through the mesh of a duck pen seemingly trying to figure out how to get in.

I walked to the front steps and looked through the screen door onto the veranda, where Rawlings's typewriter sat idle on a table. The house, built of cypress and pine, has withstood the wind, rain, and harsh sun for nearly one hundred years. Its

A fawn inspired Rawlings's Pulitzer Prize–winning book, *The Yearling*

architecture is well suited to the hot Florida climate and includes open porches, high ceilings, and plenty of windows and screen doors.

When you visit the site, bring along a picnic lunch to enjoy at the county park adjacent to the parking lot. The picnic area, which has benches and a pavilion, overlooks Lochloosa Lake. Cross Creek itself is a tiny creek that connects Lochloosa and Orange lakes.

Where: Twenty-one miles south of Gainesville on County 325 between State 20 and US 301.

Hours: The house is open Thursday through Sunday from 10:00 A.M. to 11:30 A.M. and from 1:00 P.M. to 4:30 P.M. The farm, which includes an orange grove, a yard, and a nature trail, is open from 8:00 A.M. to sunset daily.

Admission: $2.00 for adults and $1.00 for children ages six to twelve.

Best time to visit: Anytime other than August and September.

Activities: Tours of the house are given Thursday through Sunday at 10:00 A.M., 11:00 A.M., and each hour from 1:00 P.M. to 4:00 P.M. Tours are limited to ten people and are offered strictly on a first-come, first-served basis.

Concessions: None.

Pets: Not permitted, with the exception of guide dogs.

Other: The house is closed Monday through Wednesday and for the entire months of August and September. School-group tours are offered Thursdays and Fridays on the half hour between 10:00 A.M. and 11:30 A.M., with reservations necessary one month in advance. Workshops and seminars are conducted Mondays from 10:00 A.M. to 4:00 P.M., with reservations required two months in advance.

For more information:

Marjorie Kinnan Rawlings State Historic Site, Route 3, Box 92, Hawthorne, FL 32640. 904-466-3672.

OSCEOLA NATIONAL FOREST

The 188,000-acre Osceola National Forest is not as well-known as the Apalachicola and Ocala national forests primarily because it is the least developed of the three and is in sparsely populated Baker and Columbia counties, near the Georgia border in north-central Florida. Created by presidential proclamation on July 10, 1931, Osceola National Forest had been cut and heavily burned at the time. Although logging continues within the forest, wise management has helped return much of it to a natural state.

The forest, primarily pine flatwoods and cypress stands, is dotted with many swamps. The water here drains toward the St. Mary's River and Atlantic Ocean to the east and the Suwannee River and Gulf of Mexico to the west.

Hiking is one of the most popular activities in the forest. A 23-mile segment of the 1,000-plus-mile Florida National Scenic Trail passes through it. Access to this trail is provided from the Olustee Battlefield State Historic Site, 2 miles east of Olustee on US 90. The battlefield, which includes an interesting museum, is open from 8:00 A.M. to 5:00 P.M. except Tuesdays, Wednesdays, and holidays. It was the site of a Civil War battle in which Confederate troops turned back the Union army as it marched toward Tallahassee.

In several areas, the trail is blazed on old railroad trams that were used to haul timber at the turn of the century. Tram beds, elevated ridges on which cypress and pine ties may still be found, are easily recognizable.

The Osceola segment of the Florida National Scenic Trail is noted for more than twenty boardwalks that offer a good view of swamps and wetlands common to the flatwoods. Deer, gopher tortoises, wild turkeys, and red-cockaded woodpeckers inhabit the area. Facilities along the trail include campgrounds accessible from short side trails.

Other trails lead out into the Big Gum Wilderness Swamp,

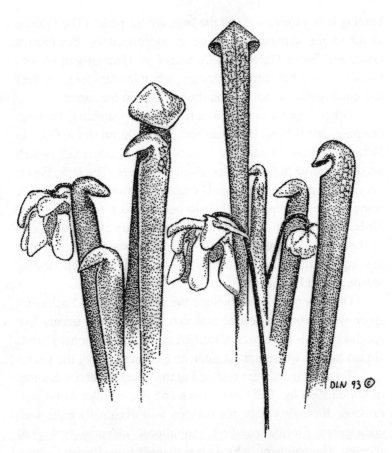

The yellow-flowering pitcher plant

a large cypress gum swamp surrounded by pine flatwoods that appears relatively untouched by humans. Anyone entering the area, which is closed to all but foot traffic, should know how to read a map and use a compass and should be prepared to be entirely self-sufficient. The swamp contains many shallow sloughs, and water usually ranges from near the surface to a few feet above.

The best months for hiking are February and March, when

hunting is at a minimum and the bugs are bearable. (They can be awful in the summer.) Hunting is supervised by the Florida Game and Fresh Water Fish Commission. General-gun season, usually November through January, when hunters look for deer and small game, is not a good time to hike in the forest.

Other popular activities here are bird watching, boating, camping, and fishing. Bird-watchers make pilgrimages to Osceola National Forest to see the red-cockaded woodpecker, which makes its home in the cavities of old pine trees. The U.S. Forest Service has painted white bands around the trunks of trees where some of the woodpeckers live to help visitors find them. The birds, which spend as long as four or five years excavating a tree to their specifications, are still difficult to spot, however. Try looking for them at sunrise and sunset or during their nesting season, April through July.

Other popular birds include the sandhill crane, Bachman's sparrow, and brown-headed nuthatch. One hundred twenty-five species of birds have been identified in Osceola National Forest, almost half of which are common at specific times of the year.

Texas cougars were released in the forest's Pinhook Swamp in March 1993 by the Florida Game and Fresh Water Fish Commission. Biologists hope the cougars will eventually mate with endangered Florida panthers, an almost identical biological species. The panthers, which once roamed from British Columbia down the East Coast of the United States, are now isolated in southwest Florida and are nearing extinction.

The Pinhook Swamp, an expansive wetland that helps form the headwaters of the Suwannee and St. Mary's rivers, is just south of the Georgia state line and lies between the Okefenokee National Wildlife Refuge and the main body of Osceola National Forest. It's not a good idea to investigate the swamp with anything other than a four-wheel-drive vehicle.

Common mammals in Osceola include armadillos, bats, bobcats, deer, gray squirrels, hogs, opossums, rabbits, raccoons, and skunks. The Shermans fox squirrel, a threatened species that can grow up to two feet tall, is distinguished by its large black head and white nose and ears. The alligator, black bear, and gopher tortoise are among the protected species here. Beavers, highly unusual for Florida, also live in the forest, sometimes building dams in culvert pipes. Biologists occasionally have to negotiate with angry property owners whose land has been flooded after water-control structures have been dammed by industrious beavers.

A good way to explore the forest is by driving into it on park roads, most of which are marked on a detailed map that can be purchased for $3.00 from the Fastway Food Store on US 90 in Olustee. The map is far more accurate than the one given away at the visitors center and is very useful in reaching many of the eight primitive hunting camps set up throughout the region. Roads are mostly hard sand but can be soft or washed out in places.

Roads lead through a series of longleaf pine flatwoods and swamps. Ponds along the roads or just back from them are popular among fishermen looking for panfish and largemouth bass. Freshwater licenses, which can be acquired in Olustee, are required.

The route I took, at the suggestion of a ranger, led from Still Road (across from Lake City Community College) to Forest Roads 236, 237, 234, 272, 212, 232, and 250. It gave me a glimpse of a good cross section of the environment. I saw squirrels, raccoons, a southern black racer, great white herons, and a coyote during the course of the 2.5-hour drive. The coyote, seen at sunset as it trotted across Forest Road 232, was the first I've come across in Florida.

The two primary recreation areas within the forest are Olustee Beach and Ocean Pond Campground, both on US 90 near Olustee. The beach, open for day use only, has a bathhouse equipped with showers, toilets, and changing areas; fire rings and grills; shaded picnic benches; and a pavilion. It also has a white-sand beach, a boat ramp, and a short pier with a man-made fish-attracting device (submerged brush piles with automatic fish-feeding mechanisms) within casting distance. A parking fee of $1.00 must be deposited in a self-service payment box on the short side road (Forest Road 231) that leads to the beach.

When I visited on a warm weekend in March, only one person was sunbathing on the beach, and there were a half dozen fishing boats on the 1,760-acre natural freshwater lake. Anglers reported little luck that day, although the lake is said to contain a healthy population of largemouth bass, bluegills, catfish, pickerel, and speckled perch.

Ocean Pond Campground, the only developed facility in the forest, is a ten-minute drive from the beach on the same lake. Some of its fifty sites are directly on the water, making it possible for boaters to moor their vessels within a few feet of their tents or trailers. All sites have concrete benches and a fire ring. They are spacious and nestled among tall pines. Water, bathrooms, and hot showers are handy, but there are no electrical hookups. The campground also has a small swimming area with a white-sand beach.

The campground was only about one-third full when I visited. That's a pity, because spring can be a good time to camp here. Frogs looking for a mate begin calling in the early evening, and birds sing all day long to mark their territory and attract a mate. Wildflowers bloom, turtles lay eggs, birds nest, turkeys gobble, and black bears prowl about looking for food.

Small animals crashed around in the thick underbrush near my tent, and armadillos and opossums seemed unconcerned as I sat at a picnic bench after dark. The campground, one of the more pleasant I've stayed at, gave me the feeling of being deep in the forest while also providing a few amenities.

Where: Approximately twelve miles east of Lake City on US 90 or sixty miles west of downtown Jacksonville on the same road.

Hours: The lone visitors center at the Osceola Ranger District Station in Olustee is open from 7:30 A.M. to 4:00 P.M. weekdays.

Admission: The only fees charged are for camping at Ocean Pond Campground ($5.00) and parking at Olustee Beach ($1.00 for cars, $5.00 for commercial buses).

Best time to visit: February through August.

Activities: The Ecosystem Trail, a one-mile interpretive loop walk, begins at Mount Carrie, several miles west of the visitors center on US 90. A butterfly and hummingbird garden is located on Park Road 250 where it converges with the Florida National Scenic Trail and another at the southeast border of the Big Gum Swamp Wilderness. Horseback riding trails are located around the West Lookout Tower in the Greenfield area. No regularly scheduled ranger-led activities are offered, but groups of eight or more can be assigned a guide if they inquire well in advance. Ranger-led programs may be added in the future at Ocean Pond.

Concessions: None.

Pets: Allowed on a six-foot leash except in swimming areas. Guide dogs are allowed in all areas.

Other: Maps and literature, including lists of plants and animals, are available at the visitors center. Groceries and camping supplies are sold at a convenience store on US 90 in Olustee, a few miles from the campground. Fishing and hunting supplies are sold a few doors down from the convenience store.

For more information:

Osceola National Forest, P.O. Box 70, Olustee, FL 32072. 904-752-2577.

OCALA NATIONAL FOREST

When I was a boy, Ocala National Forest was a magical place for me. It seemed dark and scary, and I envisioned a bear lurking behind every tree. When I looked at the forest through an adult's eyes for the first time last spring, I saw something entirely different. It wasn't impenetrable, and, sadly, it didn't look much like a forest.

Perhaps my perception was skewed. I had visited Apalachicola and Osceola national forests within two weeks of stopping here. Neither attracts as many visitors or as much commercial logging, so they appear relatively untouched. But at Ocala, I found myself looking for the forest while driving on major roads that run right through it. It wasn't until I took some side roads and visited a few recreation areas that I felt even slightly in touch with the environment.

More than 52 million board feet of timber were harvested from Ocala in 1992, four times as much as at Apalachicola and nearly six times as much as at Osceola. Although this timber came from only 1 percent of the acreage at Ocala, the cumulative effect of continued logging is noticeable.

I encountered other disappointments as well. The exhibits in the visitors center on State 40 in Silver Springs are excellent and stimulate much interest. But the individual greeting guests was less than enthusiastic when queried about the forest's attributes and seemed to know little about Alexander Springs, where I had swum as a kid. He shrugged when I asked whether it was a popular area among visitors and nearly dissuaded me from going there.

Having to purchase leaflets with basic visitor information was irritating. These are provided free at every other local, state, and federal preserve I toured. However, Ocala does have a larger inventory than most places.

Seeing a concessionaire at Juniper Springs selling peanuts as squirrel food (it's labeled that way on a sign) was disturbing. Encouraging that conduct is inappropriate, as most people are unable to differentiate between feeding squirrels and feeding other wildlife — and that promotes unhealthy behavior on the part of animals. For example, while I was walking on a nature trail at

Juniper Springs, one of the busiest places in the forest, I was accosted by two young raccoons that obviously had grown accustomed to handouts. They climbed out of a creek bed and onto a bridge and reached toward me with hands outstretched as I took a picture. They were cute but not acting as wild animals should.

Those aggravations aside, Ocala remains an attractive destination for outdoor recreation. The forest drew more than 2 million visitors in 1992, better than double that of Apalachicola and Osceola combined. Activities offered include bird watching, boating, camping, canoeing, diving, fishing, hiking, horseback riding, hunting, picnicking, swimming, target shooting, and waterskiing.

The Ocala National Forest, established in 1908, covers more than 430,000 acres in North Florida. It is the oldest national forest east of the Mississippi River and the southernmost in the nation, and it supports a variety of animals and environments.

Begin a trip to the forest with a stop at the visitors center near Silver Springs. The displays detailing the logging industry and wildlife are excellent. Life-size dioramas depict the bald eagle, barred owl, black bear, bobcat, Carolina wren, eastern cottontail, eastern indigo snake, gray fox, great blue heron, northern cardinal, osprey, peninsula cooter, red-tailed hawk, rufous-sided towhee, Shermans fox squirrel, American kestrel, turkey, and yellow-bellied sapsucker.

The bear display (a mother and two cubs) was created using victims from different road kills. Approximately 200 bears inhabit the forest, and collisions with vehicles are common at night. Another accident victim had been found along the road the day before I visited in April. A shy creature that feeds primarily on plants and berries, the Florida black bear is occasionally seen crossing the road at twilight. Statewide, the population has fallen so low that hunting black bears is banned in all but two counties in North Florida.

Wildlife surveys of the forest done in 1992 estimated populations of 8,826 white-tailed deer, 300 turkeys, 11 active colonies of endangered red-cockaded woodpeckers, and 37 active bald eagle nests. The forest's bird list includes 219 species, more than 60 of which are considered abundant or seasonally common. Bird-watchers come here primarily to see the threatened Florida scrub jay and Bachman's sparrow, but the bald eagle, red-cockaded woodpecker, sandhill crane, and American kestrel are also of interest.

Endangered bald eagles nest in the forest from November through May, with peak activity from December through April. In 1992, biologists monitored eighty nests, slightly fewer than half of which were active. About twenty-five fledglings are produced each year, although the figures for 1993 were a little lower because of damage caused by a winter storm in March. The area around Lake George is the most likely place to see eagles.

The Florida scrub jay, dependent on a variety of scrub oaks for nesting and food, was designated a threatened species by the U.S. Fish and Wildlife Service in 1987 because its range has been greatly reduced by development and agriculture. In Ocala, the jays congregate primarily in regenerated scrub areas where longleaf pines were harvested in the previous ten to twelve years.

Ocala is home to a year-round population of sandhill cranes and is a winter stopping place for many more. Although not as common as in Paynes Prairie State Preserve near Gainesville, they are sometimes seen at Mud Lake north of County 314 and at Church Lake, off State 40 about one mile east of the visitors center near Silver Springs. Sandhill cranes are a threatened species in Florida.

The same is true of the American kestrel, a robin-size falcon threatened by loss of cavity trees and reduced habitat. More than 200 nesting boxes have been constructed for kestrels in recently cut areas of sand pines and open longleaf pine communities with a grassy understory. The kestrels, which hunt grasshoppers, lizards, and small mammals and reptiles, need cavities for nesting but have no tools to make their own. They take over cavities excavated by woodpeckers and common flickers.

In 1992, the U.S. Forest Service documented eleven colonies of endangered red-cockaded woodpeckers in Ocala. The woodpeckers nest only in old, living pine trees and have declined significantly because most older timber stands in Florida are being harvested. Some of the trees containing active nests at Ocala are marked with a white band around the trunk to help people identify them. A good area to look for woodpeckers is at the intersection of Forest Road 88 and County 314 near Lake Kerr.

Like many visitors, I made the Juniper Springs Recreation Area, located sixteen miles east of the visitors center on State 40, my first stop in the forest. Swimming and canoeing are the most popular activities at Juniper Springs, one of the oldest and best-known national forest recreation areas in the East. Swimming is permitted in the spring itself, from which 13 million gallons of 72°F water flow every day. No lifeguard is on duty, but changing areas and showers are provided. The swimming hole, developed by the Civilian Conservation Corps in the 1930s, is surrounded by a concrete wall and has a fenced portion for young children at one end. The spring is wonderfully clear and slopes from a depth of 4.5 to about 20 feet.

The Juniper Creek Canoe Run begins behind the old mill adjacent to the swimming area. You can rent a canoe from a concessionaire, but get there early or be prepared to be turned away. Prepaid reservations (cash or personal checks) are accepted up to two weeks in advance. Payments for canoe rentals on-site must be in cash.

The creek begins as a winding, fast-moving stream scarcely wider than the canoe itself but broadens as it flows downstream until it is several hundred feet wide. You may see deer along the banks in the early morning and late in the day. The trip is seven miles one way and takes three to five hours. Many people pack a lunch and spend the whole day poking along. Disposable containers, bottles, and canned drinks are not allowed on the creek, so you must bring thermos jugs and pack food in sealable, reusable containers.

A lovely, three-quarter-mile self-guided nature trail begins near the canoe-launching site and runs along Juniper Creek. Juniper Springs is part of the only subtropical forest in the continental United States, and immense moss-draped oaks, statuesque palms, and ferns are common.

Raccoons wade in streams along the nature trail, and squirrels scurry up the trunks of trees. The vegetation is lush, with sabal palms, red maples, live oaks, and tall white bay trees forming a canopy over the path.

The trail ends at Fern Hammock Spring, where you can see the water bubbling up through tiny cracks in the bottom. Schools of bluegills and many largemouth bass inhabit the crystal-clear spring, where swimming and wading are prohibited.

Seventy-nine sites in three camping areas accommodate tents, trailers, and motor homes up to thirty-five feet long. All spaces are available on a first-come, first-served basis, with no reservations accepted. The sites have benches, grills, and access to water, but they have no electrical, water, or sewer hookups. The cost varies from $10.60 to $12.72 per night depending on the site. Camping supplies, firewood, charcoal, pizza, sandwiches, soft drinks, snorkels, and masks can be purchased at a concession stand at Juniper Springs.

My next stop was Alexander Springs, the place I loved most as a kid. Located off County 445 six miles from where it intersects State 19, this is Florida's finest natural swimming hole. The recreation site features a mammoth spring that spews forth 80 million gallons of water every day.

A pier extended out to near the spring's boil when I visited as a boy, but it has since been torn down. Now divers, snorkelers, and swimmers have to forge their way out from the white-sand beach.

The spring itself is twenty-six or twenty-seven feet deep, and the water seems much colder than the actual year-round temperature of 72°F. The clarity of the water also makes it seem much shallower.

It is quite common to see alligators (sometimes uncomfortably big ones) in the water adjacent to the swimming area. They are usually wary of humans and show little interest in bathers, although several that had grown used to handouts and therefore increasingly bold were removed right before my visit.

The beach, which is bordered by a shady picnic area, was crowded the Saturday before Easter. It is so popular from Memorial Day through Labor Day that it is best avoided. A fee of $2.00 is charged snorkelers and swimmers, and a fee of $5.00 is assessed scuba divers, who must show certification before entering the water. A lifeguard is on duty weekends from Easter through Memorial Day and daily through Labor Day.

The seven-mile Alexander Springs Creek Canoe Run starts at a canoe-launching area about one hundred feet from the beach. Alexander Springs Creek begins as a broad, shallow, slow-moving stream but is deeper downstream. The seven-mile trip takes four to five hours, but two-hour and half-day trips also are available. The upper portion flows slowly enough so that a person can paddle downstream some distance, then back to the starting point without too much difficulty.

The Timucuan Nature Trail, a 1.1-mile self-guided loop, leads from the picnic area through a variety of habitats. The trail, which highlights local vegetation used by early Indians, takes a little more than an hour to complete. You can explore an aquatic swamp, a river bottom, an oak hammock, and sand pine scrub along the way. Cypress trees, gargantuan ferns, poison ivy, sabal palms, saw palmettos, and Spanish moss are staples within this environment. Cedars, protected coonties, hickories, red buckeyes, wild grapes, and wild persimmons also grow along the path.

The campground at Alexander Springs has sixty-three sites capable of accommodating tents, trailers, and motor homes up to thirty-five feet long. Each site has a table and a grill or fire ring. All are convenient to rest rooms and water. No electrical or sewage hookups are available. Cost is $9.00 per night, and reservations are not accepted.

Fifteen other designated campgrounds within the forest also offer sites, and tenting is allowed anywhere, except during hunting season. Hunting dates are set and rules established by the Florida Game and Fresh Water Fish Commission.

Campgrounds other than Juniper and Alexander Springs include totally primitive areas with no showers or fees, secluded areas with limited facilities and low fees, and developed sites that charge from $7.00 to $15.50 per night. The most expensive is 211-site Salt Springs, the only campground in the forest that offers electricity. Hot showers are provided only at Juniper Springs, Alexander Springs, Salt Springs, Clearwater Lake, and Lake Dorr.

The campgrounds are described on maps available at the two visitors centers. Reservations are accepted only for group camping in two designated areas.

Conditions are usually conducive to hiking in the forest year-round. The Ocala National Trail, a sixty-six-mile segment of the Florida National Scenic Trail, winds through the forest and offers a real sense of solitude. Few people walk the entire distance, but many spend a few hours or days on the trail.

Picnic grounds are located throughout the forest. One of the nicer sites is at the Mill Dam Recreation Area on State 40, twelve miles east of the visitors center near Silver Springs. Mill Dam is strictly a day-use area open from April 1 through September 30.

It includes a 300-foot sandy beach on a 170-acre lake that is popular with swimmers, fishermen, and water-skiers. A $2.12 admission fee is charged for picnickers, swimmers, and people using the boat ramp. Some picnic sites are shaded by oak trees draped with Spanish moss, and all have concrete benches and raised grills. The area also has numerous water fountains, a pavilion, and rest rooms. Only four sunbathers were there the April Saturday when I visited.

Where: State 40, State 19, County 314, County 316, and County 42 are among the routes that lead directly into the forest.

Hours: The Forest Visitor Center/Bookstore in Silver Springs, fifteen miles east of I-75 on State 40, is open from 9:00 A.M. to 5:00 P.M. daily. The Forest Pittman Visitor Center, just north of Altoona on State 19, is open from 9:00 A.M. to 4:30 P.M. daily.

Admission: Prices vary from site to site. In general, most day-use recreation areas charge $2.12 to $2.25 per person per day. Camping ranges from no charge for a site without amenities to $15.50 per night for a site with electricity at Salt Springs.

Best time to visit: The peak visitor period is from Memorial Day to Labor Day, although the most popular recreation areas can be busy year-round. The quietest time is midwinter, when temperatures are generally in the sixties during the day and the forties at night.

Activities: The Ocala National Forest Interpretive Association conducts three-hour bus tours from the two visitors centers from November through May. A fee of $3.00 per person is requested to cover the cost of gasoline and payment of the driver. Groups with a minimum of fifteen people may schedule individual tours, but requests must be made thirty days in advance. Free interpretive programs are given on some Saturday nights in the amphitheater at Alexander Springs. The schedule is posted at the changing house near the swimming area.

Concessions: Canoes can be rented from concessionaires at

Alexander Springs, Juniper Springs, and Salt Springs. The cost at Alexander Springs is $19.75 per day, $14.50 per half day, and $10.00 for two hours. A driver's license and $20.00 deposit are required, and no reservations are accepted. Rental fees at Juniper Springs are $21.25 per day for a fifteen-foot canoe and $24.25 per day for a seventeen-footer. A $20.00 deposit is required, and reservations are accepted up to two weeks in advance with a cash payment or personal check. The number for reservations at Juniper Springs is 904-625-2808. The cost for a canoe at Salt Springs is $3.18 per hour or $21.60 per day. No deposit is required. Rowboats are available at Salt Springs for $10.60 per day. No reservations are accepted for canoes or rowboats.

Pets: Prohibited in swimming and picnic areas and on hiking trails. Pets must be on a leash and under control at all times in other areas. Guide dogs are always allowed.

Other: The Forest Visitor Center/Bookstore in Silver Springs has wonderful exhibits detailing the forest's history, plants, and animals. The facility has a fine selection of nature-related books and gifts including children's books, videotapes, and models. A detailed forest map ($2.00), a hiking trail map ($2.00), a canoeing map ($3.00), a rating and tubing guide ($6.95), and brochures about the forest's various recreation areas also are available.

For more information:

Forest Visitor Center/Bookstore, 10863 East Highway 40, Silver Springs, FL 34488. 904-625-7470.

Forest Pittman Visitor Center, 45621 State 19, Altoona, FL 32702. 904-669-7495.

PAYNES PRAIRIE STATE PRESERVE

I was excited about visiting Paynes Prairie because it is the only place I know in Florida where you can see wild bison. Having once tasted farm-raised buffalo meat at a restaurant in

Minneapolis, I have no doubt why the bison became nearly extinct. It was the finest steak I've ever eaten.

Bison, once native to Florida, were reintroduced to Paynes Prairie in 1975. Today a small herd roams freely on a 6,000-acre portion of the 19,000-acre preserve in southern Alachua County. Occasionally, the animals are seen from the observation tower near the preserve's visitors center, a platform at Alachua Lake, or Cone's Dike, a six-mile hiking trail that begins at the visitors center parking lot. My brother and nephew saw them on a previous trip, so my hopes were high.

I saw no bison, however, nor any wild Spanish horses. (Conquistadors brought the horses to Florida in the 1500s, and they were reintroduced to Paynes Prairie in 1985.) But I wasn't disappointed. The anticipation of seeing them fueled my desire to explore, and through that exploration, I derived great satisfaction.

Paynes Prairie lies in north-central Florida about halfway between the Atlantic and Gulf coasts in a region characterized by gently sloping hills and numerous lakes, ponds, rivers, and streams. Indian occupation of the area, named after Seminole chief King Payne, dates back to 10,000 B.C. The Native Americans lived pretty much in concert with nature, but the white settlers who followed exposed the land to a litany of commercial abuses, including cattle ranching, citrus groves, and steamship traffic along the region's rivers.

The state acquired the property in 1970 and has worked industriously to return it to its original state. Canals dug to siphon water from the prairie or to deliver storm runoff and sewage effluent to it have been eliminated or redirected to simulate the natural flow. As a result, the preserve's pine flatwoods, hammocks, and open fields have flourished, and the wildlife has prospered.

More than 750 species of plants and 350 species of amphibians, birds, fish, mammals, and reptiles have been identified

A sandhill crane feeds her chick

within the preserve. It is especially renowned for its bird life, with 237 species observed (97 regularly). The area is among the sites surveyed annually by the Audubon Society and is famous for being the major wintering ground of the eastern sandhill crane. Thousands of cranes descend on the preserve from mid-October to late November and stay until March. At times, hundreds can be seen along the La Chua Trail.

Threatened Florida sandhill cranes, a subspecies of the northern or greater sandhill crane, spend their entire lives in the prairie basin. Only twenty-five or thirty breeding pairs exist in the preserve today. Large birds with seven-foot wingspans, sandhill cranes are easily recognized by their resonant, trumpetlike call. The sound, similar to a French horn's, emanates from a five-foot windpipe and can be heard for up to two miles.

Other species that generate inquiries include the bald eagle, osprey, marsh hawk, red-tailed hawk, red-shouldered hawk, several wading birds, winter waterfowl, and migratory songbirds. Eagles and ospreys are primarily observed around the preserve's major bodies of water and at nearby Newnans and Lochloosa lakes. About a half dozen active eagle nests were identified within the preserve in the spring of 1992. Hawks are seen almost daily soaring over the prairie basin. Herons, egrets, ibis, and wood storks can be observed from hiking trails that cut through the marsh. Songbirds such as the blue grosbeak, bobolink, indigo bunting, and palm, parula, and prothonotary warblers are plentiful around the visitors center in the spring.

The search for bison brought me to Cone's Dike, a six-mile trail that begins in a mixed forest and continues through open range. You must pass through a gate – and read warnings about the unpredictable behavior of bison and wild horses – to get from one habitat to another.

I nearly stepped on a fifteen-inch garter snake a few yards in front of the gate. The snake was sitting motionless in the path. It tolerated being petted several times before slithering off into the grass.

Tiny purple wildflowers were growing along the ground next to the trail, and white wildflowers were clinging to a fence that separates the preserve from a neighboring cattle ranch for the first several hundred yards as it emerges into the prairie. The dike itself was dry, but the land on both sides was wet.

I walked amid colorful butterflies and watched a marsh hawk fly a few feet above the prairie several hundred yards away. At one point, I found myself staring at an eight-foot alligator in a pond on the other side of the fence.

The path became gradually wetter as the dike turned to the left and continued deeper into the prairie. The view from the dike is expansive, and topography that initially seems a monotonous blend suddenly appears to take on a variety of colors and textures. As I walked, rain began to fall, and great cloud banks streamed past.

About 1.5 miles into the walk, I came across a massive

flock of white ibis. A hundred or more of the striking wading birds took to the air as I approached but descended in the field almost as quickly. Several tall great egrets were hunting slowly in their midst, and I could see hundreds of small cattle egrets as well.

A passing jogger warned me that a large alligator was sitting in the middle of the path about a mile farther down the dike. The jogger, who runs Cone's Dike every day, advised me to steer clear because the animals can be aggressive during mating season. I came across the nine-foot alligator about twenty-five minutes later, but by then it had moved about thirty feet off the trail. It seemed uninterested as I walked past.

I started seeing more and more rain squalls forming off in the distance and behind me and decided to turn back after about four of the six miles. I looked one last time for bison before beginning the trek back. Eventually, I came across a path that seemed to lead from the dike directly across the prairie to an observation tower and decided to take the shortcut.

It was great for a while but then became increasingly wet. Soon my shoes were sinking in mud, and the water was up to my ankles. Progress was slow, but I pressed on and was rewarded for the effort: three large white-tailed deer burst across the trail less than one hundred feet ahead of me.

The path continued to about a quarter mile from the visitors center, then turned left. I took the turn and a few minutes later found myself wading through knee-deep water for about fifty yards until I got back to the dike.

Although there hadn't been any bison or horses, the alligators, birds, snake, and deer had been more than enough to satisfy me. The bison will have to wait for a future visit – and I promise I'll be back.

Hiking is perhaps the most popular activity at Paynes Prairie, which has four other designated walking trails, as well as the sixteen-mile Gainesville-Hawthorne State Trail, a rails-to-trails conversion project. Cycling is allowed along the park drive and on the Chacala, Bolen Bluff, Jacksons Gap, Cones Dike, and Gainesville-Hawthorne trails.

Horseback riding is permitted on the six-mile Chacala Trail and the Gainesville-Hawthorne State Trail. Riders must have their own horses and provide proof of a negative Coggins test. A corral is provided to assist with unloading, loading, and saddling horses, and a watering trough is located near the start of the Chacala Trail.

The Chacala Trail consists of three connecting loops. It traverses pine flatwoods, hammocks, baygall communities, and open fields and provides an opportunity to see deer, bobcats, barred owls, bald eagles, and wild turkeys. The bison and horses, I am told, are visible primarily from the Cone's Dike, Bolen Bluff, and La Chua trails. The three-mile La Chua Trail begins at the North Rim Interpretive Center and provides access to the prairie.

A half-mile trail, the Wacahoota, begins at the visitors center on the south side of the park. This shorter walk amid huge trees draped with Spanish moss is popular with children and includes a stop at a four-story observation tower.

Fishing for largemouth bass, bluegills, and speckled perch is good on Lake Wauberg. A Florida freshwater fishing license is required. A boat ramp is located on the east side of the lake, but gasoline-powered engines are prohibited.

Camping is offered in a fifty-site campground. Each site has electricity, water, a ground grill, and a table.

Barbecue grills are located in a designated picnic area and at shelters at the Lake Wauberg Recreation Area. Huge barbecue pits are strategically placed between two pavilions in the recreation area.

Where: Ten miles south of Gainesville or one mile north of Micanopy off US 441.

Hours: 8:00 A.M. to sunset year-round for day use. The visitors center is open from 9:00 A.M. to 5:00 P.M. daily.

Admission: $3.25 per car for up to eight passengers and $1.00 for each passenger beyond eight; $1.00 for bicyclists and pedestrians. Camping is $8.00 per night from June 1 through September 30 and $10.00 per night from October 1 through May 31.

Best time to visit: The weather is most pleasant in the fall.

Activities: Bicycling, bird watching, camping, hiking, horseback riding, fishing, and picnicking are the most popular activities. Ranger-led programs are scheduled on weekends from October through March. Events include free hikes, wildlife walks, bird watching, and a guided overnight backpacking trip. A fee of $5.45 per person is charged for the latter. Reservations are required for all scheduled events. Group tours are provided if arrangements are made well in advance.

Concessions: None.

Pets: Allowed on the paved drive and in parking areas if well behaved and on a six-foot, hand-held leash. Pets are not allowed on trails or in camping areas. Guide dogs are always welcome.

Other: Checklists and other written materials are available in the visitors center.

For more information:

    Paynes Prairie State Preserve, Route 2, Box 41, Micanopy, FL 32667. 904-466-3397.

DEVIL'S MILLHOPPER STATE GEOLOGICAL SITE

Devil's Millhopper is a geological wonder. Visitors descend a 232-step stairway into this lush setting to view fossilized plant life not found anywhere else in the state. Twenty million years of life is visible in this 150-foot limestone sinkhole. The site is 500 feet wide and well preserved. A creek runs through the bottom of the hole. The stairway was constructed several years ago to preserve the site, but prior to that, visitors were allowed to roam unsupervised through the sinkhole and hunt for fossils and sharks' teeth. Near the entrance to the stairway, at the rim of the sinkhole, is an exhibit area and information center.

Where: Take I-75 to State 222 east to Gainesville. It's not far from 43rd Avenue.
Hours: 9:00 A.M. to 5:00 P.M. daily.
Admission: $2.00 per vehicle, $1.00 for pedestrians or bicyclists.
For more information:
Devil's Millhopper State Geological Site, 4732 N.W. Millhopper Rd., Gainesville, FL 32606. 904-336-2008.

ICHETUCKNEE SPRINGS STATE PARK

The highlight of a visit to Ichetucknee Springs State Park is an inner-tube trip down the river, which is bordered by a hardwood hammock with a variety of plants and shrubs, including cypress, maple, longleaf pine, and oak trees. Wildlife is abundant, including wading birds, owls, fish, and turtles. River otters and limpkins also inhabit the park.

Swimming, picnicking, canoeing, and hiking are offered through the park's north entrance from June 1 through Labor Day, when the spring-fed river is open to tubers. From the north end, the tubing trip takes approximately three hours. The south entrance provides tubing from the midpoint of the river on (approximately 1.5 hours) and picnicking. Although the river is clear and you can see the bottom for most of the trip, a mask and snorkel allow you to get a good view of underwater plants and wildlife.

Inner tubes can be rented from a number of private vendors en route to the park. A tram and shuttle service is provided to transport tubers back to the entrance. On weekends and holidays, tubing is limited to 750 people per day. An early arrival is advised.

Close to half a million people visit the park each year, with most coming in June, July, and August. It's not unusual for as many as 5,000 people to pass through the gates on a weekend day in July.

Where: Eighteen miles north of High Springs on US 27.
Hours: 8:00 A.M. to sunset daily.
Admission: $4.25 per person, children under five free, at the park's north entrance, open from June through Labor Day; $3.25 per person at the south entrance, open all year.
Best time to visit: The weather is most pleasant and the crowds are most manageable in September and October and March and April. The busiest months are June, July, and August.
Activities: Canoeing, hiking, and tubing.
Concessions: Canoes, snorkeling equipment, and tubes can be rented from a half dozen vendors in the surrounding area. Food and snacks are sold at a concession stand at the south entrance.
Pets: Not recommended. They are not allowed on the river.
Other: Park brochures, maps, and hiking trail maps available at entrance station.
For more information:

Ichetucknee Springs State Park, Route 2, Box 108, Fort White, FL 32038. 904497-2511.

3
Central Florida

BLUE SPRING STATE PARK

Before the park, as you're traveling north on US 17/92, you'll pass wonderful craft and furniture stores. The crafts are all handmade, and the prices are reasonable. About one-half mile beyond the craft stores, turn left onto French Avenue and continue on to the park entrance.

The park centers on the spring and its "run" into the St. Johns River. The spring, which remains at a constant 72°F, is the winter home of nearly eighty manatees. During the winter, the manatees venture into the St. Johns River only for food, which consists entirely of sea grasses. The graceful mammals return to the warmer waters of the Blue Spring Run at night. The afternoon I was there, I counted eight manatees in the run and another three leaving the protection of the sanctuary and swimming in the St. Johns River. Manatees are an endangered species and are protected under the Endangered Species Act and the Marine Mammal Protection Act. Feeding, touching, or harassing them is illegal.

The run also is home to several alligators, turtles, and fish, including the largest gars, tilapias, and mullet I have ever seen.

Fishing within the run is not permitted, but it is allowed in the St. Johns River, where I saw several motorboats and houseboats.

Swimming and tubing are permitted in the run during the summer. The park is closed to swimming during part of the day in the winter when the manatees are in residence. In the morning,

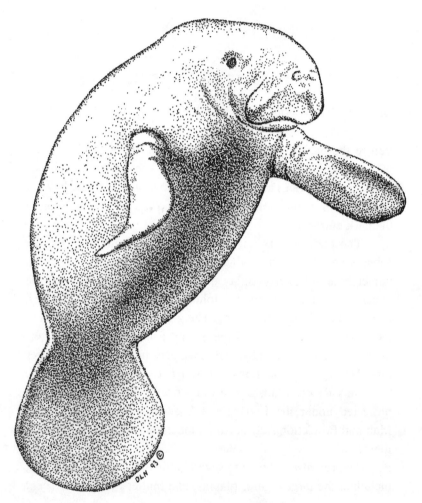

Rare manatees are protected

as the manatees swim back into the cooler waters of the St. Johns, the rangers open the swimming area closest to the point where the spring bubbles up from the aquifer below. Later in the day, as the slow-moving mammals make their way toward the river, the rangers open more swimming areas.

A boardwalk leads through mature hammocks of live and laurel oaks, wax myrtles, and sabal palms. The heart of sabal palm, also known as cabbage palm, can be eaten, but harvesting the heart kills the tree, so doing so is discouraged.

The St. Johns River was a steamboat mecca in the mid-1800s, and a rusted paddle wheel stands near the parking area as a testament to its heyday. A three-story, white-clapboard house built in the 1880s on top of a shell mound left by the Timucuan Indians has been preserved as a historic building. The first white settlers in the area built this house overlooking the river at a time when the steamboat was their only connection to the outside world.

Blue Spring is an artesian spring that travels uphill and puts forth 104 million gallons every day, making it one of the largest springs in North America. The water is always a constant 72°F.

A slide presentation on the manatee is shown three times a day in the concession building. The show features the animal's habits and behaviors, as well as its fight for survival as a species. The total manatee population in Florida is less than 2,000.

Where: Take I-4 east from Port Orange, then take US 17/92 north to Orange City. Turn left (west) on French Avenue and follow it to the park entrance.
Hours: 8:00 A.M. to sunset for day use only.
Admission: $3.25 per vehicle for up to eight people, $1.00 for pedestrians or bicyclists.
Best time to visit: To see manatees, visit the park from November through March. Swimming, snorkeling, and scuba diving are good year-round.

Activities: Camping, tubing, hiking, fishing, and canoeing.

Concessions: A camp store located near the head of the spring sells camping supplies, games, groceries, and snacks. Employees there can set you up with a canoe; a mask, fin, and snorkel set; or an inner tube. Canoe rental is $20.00 per day, and there is a limit of three people in a canoe. Seven loop canoe trails ranging from one to fourteen miles are available. Snorkeling equipment can be rented for $4.00 per hour or $10.00 per day. An inner tube can be rented for $2.00 per hour or $5.00 per day. A deposit with a major credit card or drivers license is required. Call 904-775-6888 for more information.

Pets: Not permitted.

Other: Camping facilities are available. Sites are fairly close together but well shielded by foliage.

For more information:

Blue Spring State Park, 2100 West French Avenue, Orange City, FL 32763. 904-775-3663.

904 775 -3663

HOBE SOUND NATIONAL WILDLIFE REFUGE

Hobe Sound National Wildlife Refuge is just down the street from Blowing Rocks Preserve on Jupiter Island, a narrow, sixteen-mile island between Stuart and North Palm Beach. Just driving through Jupiter Island is part of the adventure. The road to the wildlife preserve is perfectly manicured and lined with beautifully landscaped, palatial homes overlooking the Atlantic Ocean. Luckily, this is a protected area designed for golf carts, so you have an excuse to drive slowly.

The water at Hobe Beach, located just at the entrance to the refuge, is that neon blue-green color you might expect to find in the Caribbean or the Greek islands. It is clear and warm, and the sun is reflected off the white sandy bottom. A gentle slope leads slowly into the water, so on calm days, swimming is easy for children and dogs. The park is in Martin County, which allows pets on the beach as long as they are on a leash.

I brought our male cocker spaniel, Clyde, who immediately made a beeline for the waves. The park was fairly empty for a Saturday during the winter and no one seemed to mind our over-zealous fur ball. According to the ranger, if dogs are fairly well behaved and stay away from the dune, which are off-limits because of their fragile grasses and bird-nesting areas, they can even be taken off the leash a mile or so farther down the beach away from sunbathers and anglers. If you do bring a pet, be sure to bring plenty of cold water and possibly even a beach umbrella for some shade. Fresh water is not available on the beach. You'll

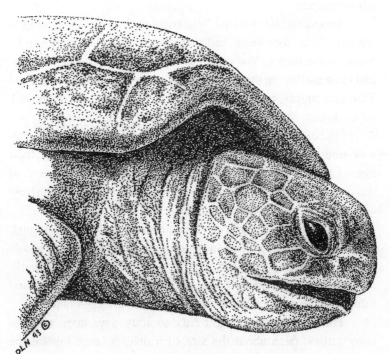

A green turtle

need to bring everything back that you take with you on your hike, as the beach has no waste drop-off sites.

Together with St. Lucie Inlet State Park, Hobe Sound National Wildlife Refuge has more than six miles of deserted beach. Sand pine scrub forests are located across the Intracoastal Waterway at the park headquarters. The refuge was established in 1969, when Jupiter Island residents donated 229 acres. Since that time, it has grown to nearly 1,000 acres.

The mainland tract is just off US 1. A nature museum is open Monday through Saturday from 8:00 A.M. to 3:00 P.M. A one-half-mile nature trail takes you through pine scrub forests down to the Intracoastal Waterway, where you can fish. In addition to the scrub pines and saw palmettos, the reserve has wild lime trees, paradise trees, live oaks, coco plums, sea grapes, and white stoppers.

Across the Intracoastal Waterway on Jupiter Island, fragile sea oats, seacoast elders, railroad vines, and beach stars can be found in the dunes. You can enjoy shelling, swimming, fishing, and even surfing on the ocean side of the refuge. On Tuesday and Thursday nights, park rangers take a small group on a dune walk to see Indian shell mounds tucked in behind the dunes.

One of the primary management goals of the park is to provide undisturbed and unpopulated areas for turtles to lay their eggs. Leatherback, green, and loggerhead turtles all make use of this area. Of Florida's six turtle species, all but the loggerhead are endangered, and it is threatened.

Beginning as early as April and lasting until July or August, adult female turtles come ashore at night. Each turtle digs a hole nearly a foot deep with her hind flippers. There she lays nearly one hundred eggs in an hour, covers the eggs with sand, and returns to the sea – never knowing whether the eggs hatch.

The eggs hatch at night fifty to sixty days later, and the baby turtles, each about the size of a quarter, race toward the ocean. The baby turtle's instincts tell it to race toward the light, which at this time of year is provided by the moon reflecting off the water. Unfortunately, in more populated areas, the baby turtles are fooled by streetlights and race away from the ocean toward busy streets.

The turtles have only about twenty-four hours to swim to a floating band of seaweed called sargassum before they lose their energy and give up. The sargassum, which originates in the Sargasso Sea, travels around the world on the edge of the Gulf Stream and provides a resting place and food for the tiny turtles.

The odds aren't good for the turtles. Birds poach the eggs, and the tiny hatchlings are easy prey for gulls and the quick ghost crab. Only a small percentage ever make it to the sargassum. People have further complicated the turtles' journey by harvesting the sargassum off the coast of the Carolinas. Even though the weed is a crucial nursery for the turtles and hundreds of other species, it is being processed and used as a filler for turkey feed.

Florida's most common sea turtle is the loggerhead, which survives mostly on crabs, shrimps, and jellyfish, including the Portuguese man-of-war. The loggerhead will keep on eating these tasty treats even if the poison from their stingers has swollen the turtle's eyes shut.

The largest of the sea turtles is the leatherback. It is less common in Florida than the loggerhead and green turtles. The leatherback, which also eats jellyfish, may grow as large as 1,300 pounds and can travel as far as 3,000 miles from its nesting place.

Where: From Florida's Turnpike or I-95, take the Jonathan Dickinson State Park exit at Jupiter. Take State 706 East to US 1 North. Follow the signs to Jupiter Island, which is across the Intracoastal Waterway on your right. Take County 707 North to Hobe Sound National Wildlife Refuge and Blowing Rocks Preserve.
Hours: Sunrise to sunset daily.

Admission: $3.00.

Best time to visit: Summer.

Activities: Swimming and hiking on a pristine beach. An interpretive center is located on the intracoastal side of the refuge.

Concessions: None.

Pets: Permitted on a six-foot, hand-held leash.

Other: Nature walks and guided tours are scheduled throughout the year and are available on request for groups. Call for details.

For more information:

Hobe Sound National Wildlife Refuge, P.O. Box 645, Hobe Sound, FL 33475. 407-546-6141.

JONATHAN DICKINSON STATE PARK

Jonathan Dickinson State Park's almost 12,000 acres make it Florida's second largest state park, and the campgrounds are often full during the winter season. Several distinct areas of the park require a lengthy stay or repeated visits to explore them fully.

The park is named for a Quaker merchant who, in 1696, was shipwrecked off the coast in the area of Hobe Sound. Dickinson and his family were among the survivors, who walked up the coast to St. Augustine. His journal describes encounters with Indians and Spanish settlers and provides much of the historical information we have about life in early Florida.

The area, logged twice before it opened as a park in 1950, also served as a U.S. Army base for instruction in radar operations from 1942 to 1944. Two of the original Army buildings are still here.

On the way into the park, head for Hobe Mountain, the highest point in South Florida. A trail leads to a tower at the top of the hill. You'll be able to see the Intracoastal Waterway and the ocean beyond Jupiter Island, as well as the Loxahatchee River and campgrounds behind you. The twenty-minute walk leads through sand pine scrub and along a ridge where threatened sand skinks, a relative of the snake and lizard, slither through the sand. The skink lives in coastal sand pine scrub, a biological community so rare it is designated "globally imperiled." Another trail, part of the Florida National Scenic Trail chain, is adjacent to the entrance parking lot and leads through thirteen miles of this threatened ecosystem. You may see a bald eagle, gopher tortoise, or Florida sandhill crane along the way.

Two loop trails are located in the concession area of the park. The Kitching Creek Trail and the Wilson Creek Trail are short walks through cypress and maple wetlands and pine flatwoods. You may hear several birds, including the threatened scrub jay and a variety of woodpeckers and bobwhites. Otters often are visible from the bridge over Kitching Creek. If you are hiking the trail near dusk, you may hear raccoons, opossums, foxes, and possibly deer rustling in the cypress and pop ash stands.

The park has a heavily used picnic and pavilion area at the end of the long entrance road. The day I was there, several Girl Scout troops were having a picnic and playing volleyball. This area includes a concession stand, grill stands, picnic benches, and a boat ramp on the Loxahatchee River. Rangers at the concession stand will take care of canoe rentals or book you on the *Loxahatchee Queen*, a thirty-passenger riverboat that tours the river — Florida's first to be named a National Wild and Scenic River.

Canoeing is a popular way to explore the park. Rangers suggest a round-trip paddle upriver to the Trapper Nelson Interpretive Site. Here you will see a cabin tucked away in the pines along the stream. Trapper Nelson was a loner who came to live on the shore of the river in approximately 1936. During the thirty-eight or so years he lived here, he became a local legend — "The Wild Man" of the Loxahatchee. You'll see the trapper's cabin, extensive woodpiles, a water tower, and a chikee (stilt house). The site also includes alligator pens, snake pits, a gopher tortoise pen, and other animals. It is open Wednesday through Sunday from 9:00 A.M. to 5:00 P.M.

On the way to Trapper Nelson's, the canoe trail leads upstream through wild territory. You'll pass red mangroves, pine trees, and a cypress forest on your way past the terminus of Kitching Creek. You may see bald eagles and ospreys nesting along the river, and strangler figs and pond apples hang over the water. Alligators are common, and rangers occasionally spot raccoons and bobcats.

Camping is popular at the park, and reservations are encouraged. Reservations are accepted over the phone for the 135 sites located in an Australian pine stand. The sites are fairly close together and crowded on winter weekends. Several air-conditioned cabins set away from the pine stand might be available. (The cabin program was being reconsidered when I visited the park.) Three primitive campsites are located in the middle of a segment of the Florida National Scenic Trail that intersects the park just west of the entrance.

Horseback riding is another popular way to see the park. Open-air stalls and a horse trail are offered. It's common to see dozens of horses walking through the pine and palmetto forests on weekends. Proof of a negative Coggins test is required before entry into the park.

The park has a bird list of 143 species, including the endangered wood stork, roseate spoonbill, peregrine falcon, smoothbilled ani, and many other endangered and threatened species. The bird list is available at the park headquarters.

Where: Take I-95 to exit 59A east in near Jupiter. Take Indian Town Road (go east) seven miles to US 1 north. Follow US 1 for five miles to the park entrance on the left.
Hours: 8:00 A.M. to sunset daily.

Admission: $3.25 per vehicle for up to eight people; $1.00 for pedestrians or bicyclists; $14.00 plus tax for a campsite, $2.00 additional for electricity.

Best time to visit: Fall, spring, and winter.

Activities: Hiking, biking, canoeing, camping, and fishing.

Concessions: Camp convenience store and canteen. The store at the main picnic area takes reservations for canoe and cabin rentals. Canoes are available for $6.00 per hour or $22.00 per day for two adults from 9:00 A.M. to 3:45 P.M. Wednesday through Sunday. The cabin concession is under review and may not be offered in the future. Call the concessionaire (407-746-1466) for more information.

Pets: Permitted on a six-foot, hand-held leash except in the camping area and near the river. Canoeing with a dog is inadvisable because of the threat posed by alligators.

Other: A ten-year old boy was recently killed in an alligator attack during a canoe trip to Trapper Johns. The boy had gotten out of the boat to clear a log out of the way.

For more information:

Jonathan Dickinson State Park, 16450 S.E. Federal Highway, Hobe Sound, FL 33455. 407-546-2771. Please send a self-addressed, stamped envelope.

BLOWING ROCKS PRESERVE

The Nature Conservancy protects this 113-acre stretch of beach donated by a group of concerned Jupiter Island residents in 1969. The preserve has unusual Anastasia limestone rock ledges where, on rough days, the water rushes through caverns in the limestone and erupts like giant saltwater geysers. The outcroppings are the largest on the East Coast and represent a Pleistocene "cliff" formed by the gradual accumulation and cementation of marine sediments. Wave action and shifting sands have carved fissures and solution holes. During high tide and winter storms, seas breaking against the rocks force tons of water skyward through these "blowholes," resulting in magnificent plumes.

The day I was here, the weather was hot and calm. The bright blue water was warm, and only a few swimmers and hikers were inspecting the rock ledges. We had the preserve almost entirely to ourselves.

A boardwalk winds through four distinct plant communities: ocean dune, coastal strand, interior mangrove wetland, and tropical coastal hammock. Interpretive brochures and placards along the boardwalk describe the plant life and tell the story of turtle reproduction. Crucial beach plants, including sea oats, the endangered beach star, railroad vine, and seacoast elder, grow in dunes protected by fences and the boardwalk. This is a critical nesting area for green, leatherback, and loggerhead turtles. The bay side of the preserve is an important natural winter habitat for West Indian manatees. Blowing Rocks Preserve also provides an important habitat for aquatic birds, including the common brown pelican, great blue heron, and osprey.

The park has an aggressive native-plant restoration project on the bay side. Volunteers and local Nature Conservancy guides work together to remove exotic pest plants such as the tenacious Brazilian pepper, Australian pine, and melaleuca and replace them with plants that would normally be found in this type of habitat. These pest species, which were introduced to the area, displace native vegetation, disrupt crucial habitats, drain aquifers of fresh water, and are not able to withstand Florida's dramatic climatic conditions, including frequent high winds and occasional hurricanes. A plant rescue group saves native plants from other sites in the area and relocates them to the preserve.

Where: From Florida's Turnpike or I-95, take the Jonathan Dickinson State Park exit at Jupiter. Take State 706 East to US 1 North. Follow the signs to Jupiter Island, which is across the

Intracoastal Waterway on your right. Take County 707 North to Hobe Sound National Wildlife Refuge and Blowing Rocks Preserve.

Hours: 6:00 A.M. to 5:00 P.M. daily.

Admission: Free to the public.

Best time to visit: Before or after a storm and May through October.

Activities: Boardwalk through coastal habitat with endangered pioneer dune plants. The beach has unusual Anastasia limestone outcroppings.

Concessions: None.

Pets: Not allowed.

Other: Suggest donation of $3.00 per person. For membership information, write or call.

For more information:

Blowing Rocks Preserve, P.O. Box 3795, Sequesta, FL 33469. 407-575-2297.

FORT DE SOTO COUNTY PARK

Because Fort De Soto is so close to two major cities (Tampa and St. Petersburg) and their suburbs, the 900-acre park is very popular. Park officials estimate that nearly 3 million people visit the park each year. Still, at certain times of the year and in several places, the park offers visitors a welcome escape from the rush of the Tampa–St. Petersburg area.

The park is made up of five islands connected by State 679. Madelaine Key, St. Jean Key, St. Christopher Key, Bonne Fortune Key, and the main island, Mullet Key, encompass 900 acres with more than seven miles of beach or bay frontage. Although St. Jean and St. Christopher keys offer 235 campsites and Madelaine Key has an 800-foot boat ramp and parking areas, most of the day-use activities are on Mullet Key.

The campsites are separated from neighboring sites by a thin wall of native vegetation, and electricity and water are available. Laundry and shower facilities are located nearby. The campgrounds are 100 percent occupied from January through April, and reservations are not accepted over the phone. Advance reservations must be made in person at one of three reservation offices: Fort De Soto County Park, daily from 8:00 A.M. to 9:00 P.M., 813-866-2662; Clearwater Office, 631 Chestnut Street, Monday through Friday from 8:00 A.M. to 5:00 P.M., 813-462-3347; St. Petersburg Office, 150 Fifth Street North, Room 146, Monday through Friday from 8:00 A.M. to 5:00 P.M., 813-892-7738. Personal checks are not accepted. A two-night minimum stay is required.

Mullet Key is shaped like a bent arm jutting out into the Gulf of Mexico. At the "elbow" of the arm sits a historic fort built in 1898. From the Gulf side, the fort looks like just a grass-covered knoll. A flight of stairs leads up to the top of the knoll, where you can look down into the bulwark below. The stairs lead to a path that runs along the top ridge of the fort — undoubtedly where soldiers kept their watch. Down below are barracks and common rooms laid out in a semicircle onto an expansive lawn. The fort has some unusual weaponry, daily interpretive tours, and a living history volunteer on weekends.

Near the fort, the county has built a 1,000-foot fishing pier, a concession stand where you can buy bait and tackle or arrange for fishing charters, and a restaurant. Fish caught in the Gulf include sea trout in the grass flats and redfish, snook, and flounder near the flats and oyster beds. A plaque near the building details the fishing regulations and size and quantity limits. Another pier a little farther down stretches out 500 feet into Tampa Bay. A concession area here sells bait, tackle, food, and other supplies.

The rest of Mullet Key is divided into swimming, parking, and picnic areas. Several picnic areas face Mullet Key Bayou, the waterway along the interior part of the "arm." This strip of mangrove-covered shoreline is a particularly good spot for bird watching as it is one of the least popular areas of the park. Several individual picnic and barbecue sites are carved out of the wooded area banking the bayou, and some sites have easy access to the water, where cormorants, herons, egrets, and other birds can be seen. Because of the park's location along the Northeast flyway, it boasts a bird checklist with 283 species, with most of the transitory birds being spotted in April.

I visited the park on a cold, overcast, blustery March Sunday. The sky was gray and the water quite rough. Only a few brave souls were out on the beach playing Frisbee with their dogs. No rangers were around, and the concession areas were closed, so dogs and people walked together freely along the beach dodging waves and taking in the fresh air. It was very peaceful.

Where: Off I-275, just northwest of the Skyway Bridge in St. Petersburg. Take exit 4 westbound on State 682. Turn left (south) on State 679 and continue across the causeway and several small islands to the park.

Hours: Sunrise to sunset.

Admission: Entrance to the park is free, but road tolls on Cunningham Key (State 679) total eighty-five cents. The year-round fee for camping is $16.50 per night, which includes tax and electricity.

Best time to visit: Spring and summer for the beach; winter for camping and seeing the fort; early March through mid-May and late fall for bird watching.

Activities: Picnicking, beachcombing, sunbathing, water sports, camping, bird watching, and fishing.

Concessions: A restaurant, three concession buildings, and two bait shops.

Pets: Dogs are permitted in the park on a six-foot, hand-held leash, but not on the beach or piers or in the campgrounds.

Other: Check with park headquarters for a list of interpretive programs.

For more information:

Fort De Soto County Park, 3500 Pinellas Bayway South, Tierra Verde, FL 33715. 813-866-2484. Please send a self-addressed, stamped envelope.

HIGHLANDS HAMMOCK STATE PARK

Highlands Hammock State Park was a park before the state even had parks, thanks to the foresight of a few concerned citizens in 1931. Four years later, the park was named one of Florida's four original state parks. Consequently, this park offers a rare chance to explore pristine, virgin cypress swamps and hardwood forests. The park's 4,694 acres began with a donation of 3,800 acres by Margaret S. Roebling, a naturalist who loved Florida fauna, saw the hammock from an airplane, and bought the property. She was concerned that the hammock might be turned into farmland. At several locations throughout the park, exceptionally large oak trees, some as old as 1,500 years, are dedicated to Roebling and her family. Currently, the state and the Friends of Highlands Hammock are trying to acquire two more parcels, one encompassing 3,200 acres.

The park was a camp for the Civilian Conservation Corps (CCC) and each year hosts a CCC festival attended by former members and their families. A museum built by the CCC just west of the entrance tells the story of this group and how they helped establish the United States' park system. The CCC also built a concession building, Bailey's Camp Store, where you can sit by a roaring fire in the winter or relax in one of the many rockers that line the front porch.

When you arrive at the park, be sure to get tickets for the tram ride, which operates at 1:00 P.M. daily except Monday and at 1:00 P.M. and 2:30 P.M. on Saturday and Sunday. The ride begins at the concession area parking lot and goes through the various plant habitats, including a virgin cypress swamp, pine flatwoods, sand pine scrub, scrubby flatwoods, bay heads, and a marsh. A ranger gives a wonderful narrative of the region's history, the birth of the park, and local flora. During my tour, the ranger pulled over several times to show children the difference between a saw palmetto and a sabal palm or to tell of a strangler fig that destroyed one of the park's great oak trees. He told us that the day before, visitors had seen a humorous encounter between a feral hog (the result of a wild boar's mating with an escaped farm pig) and an armadillo. Although we didn't have such a treat, the ranger's story was amusing.

The tram takes you past eight short trails which loop back onto the main road. If a particular one catches your eye, the ranger will stop to let you off — but the short walk back to the concession area will be up to you. Or you can return to the trail after the tram ride.

The paved loop drive through the hammock is ideal for cyclists. A day-use horseback riding trail also is available for people who have their own horses. Proof of a negative Coggins test is required to bring horses into the park.

More than 150 full-service campsites are located fairly close together and sheltered by live oak trees. The southern end of the park also has several primitive campsites in a more open scrub prairie.

After the tram ride, I decided to walk the short Big Oak Trail and loop over onto the Hickory Trail, which passes by a small orange grove. The park is highly visited, so I was not optimistic about seeing much wildlife, although white-tailed deer, alligators, otters, and bald eagles are regularly seen. I had spotted the telltale rooting holes of armadillos and feral hogs in the concession area, but I thought the chance of seeing one was small.

The Big Oak Trail leads to a huge oak tree that is more than 1,500 years old and measures 38 feet around the trunk 4 feet off the ground. Beautiful bromeliads, Spanish moss, and other air plants live in this ancient monument. The Hickory Trail intersects the Big Oak Trail via a wooden catwalk that traverses a cypress swamp, where you might hear an alligator scurrying under the boardwalk. Be sure to apply every kind of bug repellent known to man. This was the worst mosquito experience I've ever had. Halfway across the catwalk, I broke into a jog to avoid these pests – and it wasn't even mating season, when the female mosquito bites.

As I rounded the corner just after the boardwalk, I heard a very loud tapping. As I continued on, I saw that the noise was coming from a large (maybe fifteen inches tall) pileated woodpecker chiseling away some bark in search of carpenter ants or wood-boring beetles. As I got closer, frantic to remain a moving target for the bloodthirsty predators flying behind me, the woodpecker flew away, and I heard the very distinctive snorting of what I imagined to be a large, flesh-eating feral hog. I jumped up on a nearby bench and stood absolutely still, straining to hear past the pounding in my chest to determine where the wild boar was.

By now the mosquitoes were on their second quart of blood, but any movement – even the swish of my hand to get them off my face – might give away my location. Finally, I saw it. The object of my fear weighed less than ten pounds. Two more little piggies followed. They were adorable. I hopped off the bench and made my way toward the babies. Then I remembered that there was probably a very protective mother nearby, and I hopped back up to safety. But the mother didn't seem to be within earshot. When the pigs saw me, they ran to a tree stump and stood with their back ends to me. I could see them quite plainly, but as long as they couldn't see me, I suppose they thought they were safe. As I approached them, they ran squealing into the swamp.

Where: State 27 just north of Sebring.

Hours: 8:00 A.M. to sunset daily.

Admission: $3.25 per vehicle for up to eight people, $1.00 for pedestrians and bicyclists. Camping from April through November costs $8.00 plus tax. Winter camping is $13.00 plus tax. Electrical hookups are $2.00.

Best time to visit: November through April. The bugs are a serious problem in late summer.

Activities: Camping, hiking, tram ride, and interpretive center.

Concessions: Bailey's Camp Store.

Pets: Not allowed.

Other: The tram ride runs at 1:00 P.M. daily except Monday. During busy times, rangers may add another ride. Call for details. Tickets for the ride cost $1.50 and can be purchased at the park entrance.

For more information:

Highlands Hammock State Park, 5931 Hammock Road, Sebring, FL 33872. 813-385-0011. Please send a self-addressed, stamped envelope.

LAKE KISSIMMEE STATE PARK

Lake Kissimmee State Park is one of my all-time favorite places. It has something for everyone and always offers things to do to keep you entertained.

My day in the park began with a visit to the "Cow Camp," a reconstruction of an 1876 camp for cowherds. The herders would use the camp, basically an oversize chikee (stilt house) with an open-pit fire, on their way across Florida to St. Petersburg, where the cows would be loaded onto sailboats and shipped to Cuba. The reconstructed camp is staffed by a ranger who dresses in period clothes and delights anyone within earshot of tales of life in old Florida. The cowpoke will pretend not to know anything of today's world, so questions about modern conveniences will fall on deaf ears, but he will invite you to a supper of beans and dried beef — a typical meal for the cowherd. The camp is located just to the right of the main entrance road. The park's lean scrub cows, descendants of Spanish cattle from Andalusia, and wild horses graze over more than 200 acres of the park.

To get to the camp, walk 500 yards or so down a path through a prairie hammock. This habitat occurs on elevated ground along the edge of prairies and is characterized by a dense canopy of live oak trees with an open, prairielike understory. Passing underneath one ancient oak, I heard the buzz of what sounded like a chain saw in the distance. I stopped to listen, then walked cautiously forward. The sound grew louder as I approached a very large oak branch hanging over the path. In the crook of the branch, a thousand or more honeybees were busy at work. I kept walking slowly and quietly, with my hands at my sides, as I passed below their swarm unharmed.

It is not surprising to find honeybees in this region of Florida. The area surrounding the park is practically all citrus groves. In fact, Camp Mack Road is lined with orange trees, and in the spring, bees are busy pollinating the sweet-smelling blossoms. These bees have more important things to do than sting people, so as long as you don't interfere with their work, you'll be fine.

After spending some time listening to the cowpoke's oral history of Florida, I returned back to the parking area just outside the camp. This time, I walked with some bird-watchers down the service road instead of taking the path. We saw many birds taking advantage of the shade and protection of the ancient oak hammock. Among them were pileated, red-bellied, and downy woodpeckers; Carolina wrens; cardinals; rufous-sided towhees; summer tanagers; catbirds; bobwhites; mockingbirds; blue jays; pine warblers; and eastern meadowlarks.

A dead, hollowed-out oak tree looked like the perfect home for an owl. First we heard the barred owl cry, "Who cooks for you?" Then we spotted the owl sitting high in a tree. When we got closer, we could see that this was a baby barred owl – its downy feathers still fluffy and full. The baby was tired and wasn't accustomed to being awake at this hour of the day. We could see its long eyelashes blinking as it tried to keep a watchful eye on us.

We walked on and spied one of the baby's parents. Then, in a tree only fifteen feet away from where we had been standing, we spotted a bald eagle. It had been there the whole time as we'd talked, laughed, and pointed out other birds. It looked at us for a second or two and then flew off. Watching this majestic bird take to the air was quite a sight.

At the end of the long park drive are the concession and picnic areas. Even in the busiest season, only a few families take advantage of this park. Canoe and boat rentals are available although the concessionaire had closed early on the Saturday I was here. Many local fishermen use the ramp to launch their boats. Lake Kissimmee is just a short distance from the dock, and fishing in the lake is excellent. Bass, bluegills, speckled perch, and catfish are plentiful enough to satisfy the anglers as well as the eagles, ospreys, alligators, and otters.

Lake Kissimmee is Florida's third largest lake, and along with Lake Rosalie and Tiger Lake, it forms the headwaters for the Everglades. The lake is filled with runoff from the surrounding countryside. During the rainy season, the water level may rise high enough to flood the live oak hammocks that border the lake. In fact, the weeks preceding my visit had been particularly wet, and many of the trails were swampy. When the water flows across the marsh and wet prairie, it is cleansed by the vegetation, which absorbs many of the nutrients that could cause the lake to become polluted. As the water level rises in the other lakes of this drainage system, they overflow through the marshes and small winding streams to Lake Kissimmee. The water leaves the lake from its south end through the ninety-four-mile Kissimmee

River, which travels to Lake Okeechobee. The largest of Florida's many lakes, Lake Okeechobee overflows into the Everglades.

The relatively recent history of the waterway has been riddled with controversy. In 1947, a hurricane caused serious flooding, drowning hundreds of residents and cattle on nearby ranches. As a result, the U.S. Army Corps of Engineers embarked on a ten-year canal construction project to straighten and control the waterway beginning in 1961. Seven navigational locks measuring 30 by 90 feet were installed, and canals were built to drain 45,000 acres of wetlands. Almost immediately, the waterfowl population declined by as much as 90 percent. The project left behind stagnant portions of the old Kissimmee River and water too rich in nutrients rushing for Lake Okeechobee, the Everglades, and Florida Bay. It was an ecological disaster. By 1987, Congress had approved some funding to restore this critically endangered habitat, and some progress has been made. But this progress has been much too slow, and more action must be taken soon to protect the river, the Everglades, Florida Bay, and South Florida's supply of drinking water.

The park has two backpacking trails, the 6-mile North Loop Trail and the 6.7-mile Buster Island Loop Trail. Both trails lead to primitive campsites. They traverse the park's six plant habitats: scrubby pine flatwoods, mesic pine flatwoods, wet prairies, wet pine flatwoods, a prairie hammock (or live oak hammock), and a hardwood swamp — a relatively new plant community in the park caused by the low water level of Lake Rosalie for several years. The swamp displaced wet prairie and marsh. The hardwood swamp is similar in some respects to the live oak hammock. It has a greater diversity of plant types and is located on low, poorly drained terrain.

The park also has sixty full-facility campsites and two large bathhouses closer to the parking and concession area. The campsites are well isolated from their neighbors and have electrical hookups for recreational vehicles. Near the campsites is an observation tower that provides a breathtaking view of Lake Kissimmee and the spreading marshland it feeds. From the tower, you can see the grasses dotted with great white herons and other wading birds.

My goal for the day was to catch a glimpse of a feral hog — considered a nuisance and an ecological disaster in parks because of their voracious rooting. Since all the trails were wet, a ranger suggested that I might see a wild boar if I hike down one of the service roads near dusk.

I drove my car as far as I could down the service road on the north side of park drive. I clumsily stumbled under the bar across the service road, turned the corner, and found myself standing among four white-tailed deer. We all stopped and looked, and since I didn't look too menacing, the deer continued

Bobcats or wildcats are seldom tamed

to eat. I was no more than fifteen feet away from them. Slowly, I walked closer, and they walked with me for another twenty or so feet. Then the distance between us started to grow as they began walking a little faster.

I sat down in the middle of the service road, and the deer turned around and began walking toward me. They were within twelve to fifteen feet of me when we heard a noise from the saw palmetto bushes by the side of the road. We looked at each other, then back toward the noise. Out of the bushes directly between us climbed a bobcat.

The bobcat saw the deer first, then turned around and saw me. We were no more than seven feet away from each other – a little too close for anyone's comfort.

The bobcat looked at me, and its eyes widened with surprise. We all stayed frozen that way for a full five seconds until I slowly started to get up and back away. When I made my first move, the bobcat ran straight ahead across my path. The deer turned tail and ran, and I made my way back to the car. Bobcats are very shy animals. The rangers had seen this one only twice before.

On my way back to the entrance, I came across an area just to the north of the gate that was teeming with threatened Florida scrub jays. These beautiful skyblue and tan jays are friendly and bold and have been known to take unshelled peanuts out of peoples hands (not a practice to promote because of their threatened status). They are beautiful to watch, and they have a loud and varied call.

If you are not camping in the park, you might consider staying at the Jacaranda Hotel, a historic stone hotel located in the center of Avon Park, only thirty-five minutes south of Lake Kissimmee State Park. The rooms and lobby have been restored to their original 1925 grandeur. The stately lobby has twenty-five-foot-high ceilings and beautiful hardwood floors. The rooms are bright and airy. Period furniture and fixtures add to the hotel's ambience. The hotel is affiliated with South Florida Community

College, and the dining room is staffed with restaurant management students. Sunday brunch offers table after table of food for
only $7.45. For reservations, call 813-453-2211.

If you arrive at the hotel too late for dinner, try Touch of
Italy, an authentic Italian restaurant nearby. A glass of wine, a
Caesar salad, a plate of vegetables, some pasta, and an entrée
will cost an average of $10.00 per person, and the food is won-
derful. 813-452-0034.

Where: Take State 60 east from Lake Wales. About nine miles
along, turn left onto Boy Scout Road. Follow this road to a stop
sign, then turn right onto Camp Mack Road. The entrance is
about five miles along.
Hours: 7:00 A.M. to sunset daily.
Admission: $3.25 per vehicle for up to eight passengers, $1.00
for pedestrians and bicyclists. Motorcycles are classified as vehi-
cles. Camping in the summer (April through October) is $8.00
plus tax and in the winter $12.00 plus tax. Electricity is $2.00
extra.
Best time to visit: Winter. The bugs are a problem in the
summer.
Activities: Hiking, camping, fishing, boating, and canoeing.
Concessions: Canoe rentals and a convenience store.
Pets: Not permitted in the camping area.
Other: A boat ramp is located near the concession area.
For more information:
Lake Kissimmee State Park, 14248 Camp Mack Road, Lake
Wales, FL 33853. 813-696-1112. Please send a self-addressed,
stamped envelope.

TIGER CREEK PRESERVE

Tiger Creek Preserve is located along the Lake Wales Ridge, the
spine of Florida and the only remaining stretch of endangered

habitat hosting more than twenty-four of the state's rarest species, including the scrub lizard, sand skink, scrub jay, pigmy fringe tree, and large-flowered Bonamia. The Nature Conservancy purchased the first 900 acres of this 4,500-acre park in 1968, but the area was recognized as an environmental treasure long before that.

As early as 1920, Edward Bok, founder of Bok Tower Gardens — a park with acres of formal and informal gardens guarded by a bell tower — recognized the area as a prized jewel and worked toward preserving the habitat. The Bok legacy continued with environmentalist and Bok Tower director Ken Morrison, after whom a trail in the north section of the park is named.

Tiger Creek and nearby Patrick Creek, both pristine blackwater streams, are the centerpiece of the ridge, which developed millions of years ago from receding ocean waters. The south end of the preserve has four major trails accessed by Pfundstein Road or Murray Road. In the north end of the preserve, five shorter trails wind along Tiger Creek. Stop in at preserve headquarters, just off Walk-in-Water Road, for trail maps and instructions.

Cooley Trail is a thirty- to forty-five-minute loop beginning just after Pfundstein Road. The trail goes through a small area of hickory and oak scrub to a point on Patrick Creek. A short side trail dead-ends in the hardwood swamp. Benches near the beginning of the trail provide a nice resting place.

Tiger Creek Preserve also contains a twelve-mile segment of the Florida National Scenic Trail. The trail starts in the south end of the preserve and winds its way north through the natural areas, then connects with the Highland Loop Trail. The Florida National Scenic Trail is a long, sandy hike that allows access to the central highlands area and goes past an overlook on Patrick Creek. The Highlands Loop Trail is a two-hour hike that leads through scrub pines and saw palmettos.

Patrick Creek Overlook is a two-hour round-trip hike that leads to a spot overlooking the creek. Access is by the Florida National Scenic Trail off Pfundstein Road.

In the north area of the preserve, the five shorter trails are Hammock Trail, Carter Hill Trail, Jenkins Trail, Cary Bok Trail, and Morrison Trail. Access to the trails is from Wakeford Road.

If possible, call ahead for guided hikes. With more than 425 species of flowering plants, nearly 150 species of birds, and various mammals, the preserve is best seen with a botanist.

Where: From Lake Wales follow State 60 approximately seven miles east. Turn left (south) onto Walk-in-Water Road. Follow it to the entrance at Wakeford Road.

Hours: Sunrise to sunset.

Admission: Free. A donation to The Nature Conservancy is encouraged.

Best time to visit: Year-round. The weather is beautiful in the spring, and bird populations are high.

Activities: Hiking and bird watching.

Concessions: None.

Pets: Not permitted.

Other: Smoking, radios, camping, firearms, and off-road vehicles are prohibited. Spectacular flora blooms from September to early November. Make sure to bring your bug repellent!

For more information:

The Nature Conservancy, 225 East Stuart Avenue, Lake Wales, FL 33853. 813-678-1551.

GREEN SWAMP WILDLIFE MANAGEMENT AREA

The Green Swamp is one of the most ecologically important areas of Florida because it is the headwaters of five major rivers (Hillsborough, Kissimmee, Oklawaha, Peace, and Withlacoochee) and the source of South Florida's drinking water. The high-elevation water pressure of Green Swamp, significant because it supplies 70 percent of the state's water, prevents saltwater intrusion from the Atlantic Ocean and the Gulf of Mexico from seeping into the web of caverns that are part of the Floridan Aquifer.

So far, the Southwest Florida Water Management District owns 54,000 acres of the swamp, and more purchases are pending. The Florida Game and Fresh Water Fish Commission manages the wildlife, and hunting is the principal activity in the park.

The gates to the swamp are open only during hunting season, but walk-ins are increasing. During the spring months, migratory birds can be seen resting here. Mammals include otters, bobcats, wild hogs, deer, and the Florida panther.

The swamp contains nineteen miles of the Florida National Scenic Trail, beginning at the access point on Rockridge Road. The trail passes through pine flatwoods, hardwood forests, cypress heads, swampland, and river floodplains. Long pants, hiking boots, long-sleeved shirts, and hats with netting are suggested. The bugs are fierce and unrelenting.

Where: Take Rockridge Road off US 98 north of Lakeland. The road is not well marked, but two convenience stores along the way will help you with directions. Green Swamp is off the beaten track, so don't worry if it seems you've gone too far.

Hours: The gates are open only during hunting season. At other times, you can hike in from Rockridge Road. Be sure to wear bright colors and stick to open paths.

Admission: Free. Licenses are required for hunting and fishing.

Best time to visit: Winter. The bugs are not as bad then, and the roads and paths are intact.

Activities: Hiking, horseback riding, backpacking, hunting, and fishing.

Concessions: None.

Pets: Not permitted.

Other: No camping facilities.

For more information:

Florida Game and Fresh Water Fish Commission, South Region, 3900 Drane Field Road, Lakeland, FL 33803. 813-644-9269.

WITHLACOOCHEE STATE FOREST

The Withlacoochee River twists through 138 miles of state forest and wildlife management areas. The river begins at the Green Swamp and winds its way to the Gulf of Mexico. Along the way lies some of Florida's most pristine country. The forest itself comrises more than 113,430 acres with diverse wildlife and habitats.

You could stay a month here and still not see everything. The 1,230-acre Headquarters Tract was formerly a Civilian Conservation Corps camp and contains McKethan Lake, a popular fishing spot. If you are going to explore the park, it is a good idea to start here. Pick up park literature, maps, hunting schedules, and restrictions. The forest map will help you when exploring other tracts.

For hiking, your choices include the 46.7-mile Citrus Trail, the 22.3-mile Croom Trail, the 6.8-mile Hog Island Trail, and the 25.3-mile Richloam Trail, among others. Some of the habitats you will pass through include dense pine forests, prairie lakes, and hardwood forests with sensitive ferns in damp ravines. The Richloam Trail is full of cypress ponds and saw palmettos. It seems to be favored by feral hogs and snakes, particularly the poisonous cottonmouth. Deer, wild turkeys, wild ponies, and cattle also can be seen along this trail.

Canoeing is another way to explore the area. During the dry season, water hyacinths and stumps may make passage difficult. Mink, otters, hawks, frogs, snakes, and alligators have been seen along the wilder areas of the river. Silver Lake, just a widening in the river within the Croom Tract, is a popular spot, and many canoeists put in here. Dogs are strictly prohibited, as the alligators along the Withlacoochee pose a serious threat to them. Several takeouts and camping areas are located along the river. Check with headquarters for their locations.

For horseback riding, the only stable in the park is located at Tillis Hill, a 215-foot hill in the Citrus Tract. The network of horse trails is blazed with blue bands and passes through sandhill scrub, oak thickets, sand pine and longleaf pine forests, and hardwood forests. This tract has an abundance of fox squirrels — two-foot-tall squirrels with fluffy tails and distinctive coloring. Some recreational activities, including hiking, are suspended during portions of the hunting season. Check with the headquarters.

The Jumper Creek Tract offers a quiet trail to hike after hunting season and in the spring. The primary mission for this area is to protect the fragile ecosystem, and birding is excellent. Several freshwater marshes support abundant wildlife. No recreation facilities are available, and hikers are encouraged to stay on the trail and leave the surrounding habitats undisturbed.

Where: Five different tracts of land are accessed through various points. The headquarters is located off US 41 in Brooksville.
Hours: Sunrise to sunset. Hiking is prohibited during several hunting seasons. Call ahead before you make the trip.
Admission: None.
Best time to visit: Winter and spring. Recreation activities are suspended during several days of hunting season in different areas. Call the headquarters for specific dates.
Activities: Horseback riding, biking, hiking, and canoeing. Of Florida's 450-plus miles of designated horse trails on public property, 106 miles are in Withlacoochee State Forest. Proof of a negative Coggins test is required. Hundreds of miles of hiking trails are contained within the park boundaries. Make sure you

have a clear copy of the forest map if you plan to do some hiking, as it is easy to get lost without one. The Withlacoochee River Canoe Trail is an eighty-four-mile run through wilderness and encroaching civilization. Check with the forest headquarters or Nobleton Canoe Outpost about the river level and conditions before heading out. Call 904-754-6777 for information.

Concessions: None.

Pets: Prohibited in recreation areas and campgrounds but permitted on trails.

Other: Campgrounds located throughout the forest range from primitive to plush. The Croom Tract has nearly 200 sites. Reservations are recommended. Camping year-round costs $8.00 per night, $10.00 with electricity.

For more information:

Withlacoochee Forestry Center, 15019 Broad Street, Brooksville, FL 34601. 904-754-6777.

4
South Florida

COLLIER-SEMINOLE STATE PARK

Collier-Seminole State Park, which borders the southwest Florida mangrove swamp and Big Cypress National Preserve, is a popular destination for campers and explorers. The 6,423-acre area includes a wealth of vegetation and wildlife typical of the Everglades region, and it's also a good base from which to explore many other environmental attractions.

The Gulf Coast Ranger Station at Everglades National Park is a thirty-minute drive from here. The boardwalk at the Fakahatchee Strand State Preserve is even closer, and so is the Rookery Bay National Estuarine Research Sanctuary. Audubon's Corkscrew Swamp Sanctuary and the Ding Darling National Wildlife Refuge are both about an hour away.

Collier-Seminole is more than just a place to pitch a tent or anchor a recreational vehicle for a few nights. Nearly two-thirds of the park is a wilderness preserve made up almost entirely of mangroves. This is both good and bad — good because the jungle-like atmosphere stimulates the imagination, bad because the mosquitoes can be fearsome. Check with the ranger station before any visit, especially in the summer.

You can explore the park's wilderness preserve by canoe

on a 13.5-mile loop trail restricted to nonmotorized vessels. Canoeists are allowed to stay overnight at a designated primitive campsite limited to five groups. You must obtain a camping permit before embarking. The cost is $15.90 per day to rent a canoe, $3.00 per person, and $2.00 for parking. A map of the wilderness is available from a ranger at the park gate.

Raccoons are the most abundant mammals in the preserve, but endangered manatees, mangrove terrapins, and mangrove water snakes also are seen occasionally in tidal creeks studded with oyster beds and sandbars. Ospreys, pelicans, and roseate spoonbills are common, and mud bars exposed at low tide are often covered with plovers, sandpipers, and other small birds.

The park itself has two trails — a 45-minute self-guided tour that ends at a salt marsh and a 6.5-mile hiking trail that winds through pine flatwoods and a cypress swamp. Walk-in camping is allowed at a designated site on the latter trail, constructed in cooperation with the Florida Trail Association. The cost is $3.00 per person per night. This trail should be attempted only in winter, as oppressive heat and deerflies make it miserable the rest of the year.

The forty-five-minute hike at Royal Palm Hammock is a better choice for most visitors. Within a few steps, you'll find yourself immersed in a botanical treasure. You'll see gumbo-limbos, Jamaica dogwoods, royal and sabal palms, buttonwoods, strangler figs, bromeliads, white stoppers, and a variety of ferns. The trip ends at an observation tower from which you can look out over a salt marsh and occasionally watch hawks and wading birds feed.

Other animals that you may see in the park include alligators, bobcats, black bears, saltwater crocodiles, opossums, raccoons, and squirrels. The endangered Florida panther is known to traverse the park in some of the most remote areas, but the reclusive cats are never seen.

A commercial operator offers seventy-five-minute boat

tours out of the park basin on the mangrove-shrouded Blackwater River. These tours are too short and not varied enough for me. Better tours, with much more to offer, are offered out of the Gulf Coast Ranger Station at Everglades National Park.

The park campground has 130 campsites, 19 of which are in a wooded area reserved for tent camping. The campground has a play area with swing sets and monkey bars, clean rest rooms, and hot showers. The sites are close enough together that you may feel cramped in the winter. An overnight stay is inadvisable in the summer, when temperatures rise above 100°F and rangers wear mosquito netting when they go outdoors.

Each campsite includes a picnic bench, grill, and water, and electricity is available. During my stay, armadillos and squirrels regularly visited me, and a red-shouldered hawk perched atop a fence post less than one hundred feet away from me for a few minutes one afternoon.

Where: Approximately ninety-three miles west of Miami and seventeen miles south of Naples on US 41.

Hours: 8:00 A.M. to sundown daily.

Admission: $3.25 per vehicle for up to eight passengers, $1.00 per person for extra passengers, pedestrians, cyclists, and groups. Camping is $8.00 per night from May 1 through November 30 and $13.00 from December 1 through April 30. Electricity is $2.00 per night extra.

Best time to visit: Winter. The mosquitoes can be bad in the spring and unbearable in the summer. Contact the park about conditions before you visit.

Activities: Ranger-led campfire programs, canoe trips, and walks are scheduled on weekends in the winter. Canoe Rentals and a boat ramp are provided. The Blackwater River flows through the park, allowing access to excellent saltwater sport-fishing in the Ten Thousand Islands region of the Gulf of Mexico.

Concessions: Seventy-five-minute boat tours of the Blackwater River cost $8.50 and leave from the basin four or five times a day. Canoes can be rented for $3.18 per hour or $15.90 per day. Inquire about them at the park gate.

Pets: Not allowed on the trails or in the camping areas, wilderness preserve, or concession areas. Where pets are allowed, they must be kept on a six-foot, hand-held leash and be well behaved at all times. Guide dogs are welcome in all areas of the park.

Other: The park has a picnic area near the boat basin, an interpretive center, and two hiking trails. A lighted, screened-in area with picnic benches is provided so that campers can escape from the mosquitoes or read at night.

For more information:

Collier-Seminole State Park, Route 4, Box 848, Naples, FL 33961. 813-394-3397.

CORKSCREW SWAMP SANCTUARY

I had taken only two steps inside Corkscrew Swamp when I saw my first bird — a barred owl perched in a stately pine. A telescope, set up by a sanctuary volunteer, made scrutinizing the bird easy.

Blue jays and crows began to harass the owl as I watched. They flew close to the owl and squawked loudly, like a mob of kids taunting a classmate on a playground. Under other circumstances, the owl might have eaten one of them, but not now. There is safety in numbers, so the harangue continued. Eventually, the smaller birds drove the predator out of the tree.

I was delighted to have observed one of nature's hazing rituals and started refreshed for the sanctuary's two-mile nature trail. But I was interrupted after only a few steps by three bobwhite quail that darted across my path. Then a gray catbird, concealed in the adjacent underbrush began to sing. And the sound

of a pileated woodpecker, as unrelenting as a jackhammer, reso-
nated through the cypress forest around me.

I am not a bird-watching fanatic, but I was fast becoming a
convert. Instinctively, I checked to make sure I hadn't forgotten
my field guide in the car.

People travel from all over the world to watch birds at
Corkscrew Swamp Sanctuary. More than 200 species have been
recorded within its boundaries, and it is not unusual to see or
hear 39 to 50 different birds on any given day.

The 10,560-acre refuge, owned and operated by the National Audubon Society, also contains the world's largest remaining bald cypress forest. Some of the trees, closely related to the
giant redwood and sequoia, are more than 700 years old, 130 feet
tall, and 25 feet around.

The 700-acre forest, saved from logging when a coalition
of conservation groups established the sanctuary in 1954, is

Florida river otters are smaller than their northern cousins

accessible via the two-mile Boardwalk Trail. Numbered stations correspond with a guidebook that you can borrow at the visitors center, and naturalists are stationed along the trail to answer questions and point out interesting birds and plants.

The scenery is so dramatic and the backdrop so inspiring that Corkscrew is the most heavily visited of all the Audubon sanctuaries. The refuge contains many threatened and endangered animal, bird, and plant species.

Many bird-watchers come specifically to see endangered wood storks, limpkins, American swallow-tailed kites, and painted buntings. The sanctuary is home to the country's largest nesting colony of wood storks, with numbers varying from year to year depending on water levels. The best time to see them is December through April or May. Limpkins, unusual wading birds that walk with a limping gait when feeding, are found year-round. American swallow-tailed kites, which have deeply forked tails and a graceful, acrobatic flight, have shown up on February 17 in each of the past three years. And buntings, one of Florida's most colorful birds, are present from November through March.

As many as a half dozen of the thirty remaining Florida panthers roam the sanctuary, and endangered gopher tortoises sometimes cross the trail near the visitors center. One of the largest black bears in South Florida occasionally navigates through the swamp's parking area. Neither that particular bear nor the panthers, which are fitted with radio transmitters, are ever seen.

Animals common along the boardwalk include alligators, armadillos, black bears, bobcats, eastern diamondback rattlesnakes, eastern indigo snakes, gray squirrels, river otters, spotted skunks, and white-tailed deer. But it is the bird life – and the quiet – that appeals to most visitors.

The trail begins in pine flatwoods. Red-shouldered hawks soar overhead, and blue jays, catbirds, and warblers congregate in the dense saw palmettos that make up much of the underbrush. Animal tracks and tortoise burrows are visible from the path.

A boardwalk begins at a wet prairie, which serves as a bridge between the dry pinelands and the cypress swamp. During summer and spring, wildflowers dot the prairie. The real fun begins when the boardwalk enters the cypress forest, which is cool and dark, like a towering cathedral. Natural wonders lurk around almost every corner.

You walk among giant cypress trees and stumps to which a wide assortment of bromeliads have become attached. Purple irises, swamp lilies, and duckweed cover the ground. Multi-colored butterflies flitter by and Carolina anoles and southeastern skinks scurry along the deck, peering back from the rails. The deep-throated croaking of alligators and frogs blends with the hammering of woodpeckers and the calls of songbirds.

In a matter of less than an hour, I saw many beautiful birds, including a broad-winged hawk; a great-crested flycatcher; a cardinal; a Carolina wren; a little blue heron; palm, parula, and pine warblers; a red-bellied woodpecker; red-eyed, solitary, and white-eyed vireos; a swallow-tailed kite; a tricolored heron; and a month-old wood stork. The baby wood stork was in a nest high up in a tree at Lettuce Lake. It wouldn't have been possible to see the bird if not for a volunteer naturalist who has a telescope aimed at the tree. Seeing the baby bird was a special moment. Because of high-water conditions, bird-watchers found only 4 wood stork nests in 1993, as opposed to 1,200 in 1992. The stork, which needs low water to concentrate fish into a confined area for it to feed, tilted its head and peered skyward as a jet roared a few miles overhead.

I returned to the visitors center after nearly 4.5 hours. As I ate lunch at the picnic area, I watched more birds. When I was done, I didn't want to leave.

Where: Twenty-five miles northeast of Naples off Immokalee Road (County 846). Immokalee Road is exit 17 off I-75. Do not

take exit 19, Corkscrew Road. The sanctuary is located in an extremely rural area on back roads, so it is best to consult a map.
Hours: 7:00 A.M. to 5:00 P.M. from December through April; 8:00 A.M. to 5:00 P.M. from May through November.
Admission: $6.50 for adults, $5.00 for full-time college students and National Audubon Society members, and $3.00 for children ages six through eighteen. Children younger than six are free.
Best time to visit: Year-round. Mosquitoes are never much of a problem, and there is always something to see.
Activities: The two-mile nature trail takes a minimum of two hours to complete. Booklets that complement the self-guided tour are available on loan at the visitors center. Naturalist-guided tours are offered for groups of ten or more, but reservations must be made a month in advance.
Concessions: None.
Pets: Not permitted.
Other: Wheelchairs and strollers are available at the visitors center at no charge. An extensive selection of field guides and other books on Florida natural history, cards, gifts, and cold drinks can be purchased here. Although food and drinks are not allowed in the sanctuary, picnic benches are provided in a well-manicured area adjacent to the parking lot. Strategically placed birdhouses allow you to watch birds while you eat. Bring binoculars, a camera, a strong sunscreen, and food and drinks for a picnic lunch.
For more information:
Corkscrew Swamp Sanctuary, Route 6, Box 1875A, Sanctuary Road, Naples, FL 33964. 813-657-3771. Please send a self-addressed, stamped envelope.

LONG KEY STATE RECREATION AREA

Most visitors come to the Florida Keys to boat, dive, fish, and snorkel, and you can enjoy all those activities here. But what makes Long Key unique is its canoe and walking trails, as well as the campsites that are directly on the ocean.

The Long Key Lakes Canoe Trail is a well-marked, 1.25-mile self-guided trail through a shallow tidal lagoon. The twenty stopping posts along the way correspond with a well-written interpretive brochure that is available at the park entrance station.

You may see small fish, ducks, hermit crabs, herons, horseshoe crabs, jellyfish, marine worms, starfish, and wading birds along the way. The trail is navigable for novices, and no portaging is necessary. Canoes can be rented at the park, and the launch site is only a few hundred yards from the ranger station. A bright blue parrot fish and three foot-long barracuda were swimming in the shallow, clear water next to the dock when I visited in May.

Although walking in a forest – a forest filled with cacti – seems an incongruous activity in such a highly developed tourist spot, don't miss the opportunity. You can park your car and jump right into a hammock.

More than 120 plants have been identified in the park. Most are visible along the 1.6-mile Golden Orb Nature Trail, a seventy-five-minute walk along the beach and over a mangrove-lined lagoon. The trip is pleasant anytime but most enjoyable in the company of a naturalist. Free, two-hour guided walks are scheduled at 9:00 A.M. every Wednesday.

The trail takes you through several distinct environments – mangrove and hardwood forests, a sandy berm, and scrub – each with its own plant community. The altitude along the trail ranges from below sea level to five feet above, with altitude determining the plant life. The demarcation between one zone and the next is easy for even a novice to recognize.

The berm – a rolling, sandy region formed by continuous winds – is among the most intriguing portions of the trail. The vegetation includes barb-wire cactus, deadly nightshade, and lantana – all of which can be harmful to your health – as well as edible offerings such as prickly pear cactus and sea grapes.

Don't even think about snacking unless you know your plants. Lantana produces an attractive purple berry that can be fatal or cause severe liver damage or extreme sun sensitivity if ingested. Deadly nightshade bears a fruit that looks like a miniature tomato. Although used to produce heart medicine and other pharmaceuticals, the fruit is deadly in its raw form.

Even those with little knowledge of plant life can appreciate the amazing variety of vegetation. It doesn't take long to realize that you are exploring a botanical treasure.

In a one-acre portion of a hammock, it is possible to see forty-four hardwood and softwood species, including cat's-claw, crabwood, gumbo-limbo, Jamaica dogwood, pigeon plum, poisonwood, ram's horn, white stopper, and torchwood. Early inhabitants burned torchwood oil, which smells like citronella, to repel mosquitoes. The mosquitoes were so severe when Spaniards first visited in the late 1490s that it was possible to be suffocated by them.

The trail also includes an observation tower and boardwalk that leads over a tidal lagoon. Wading birds use the lagoon to rest and feed and can often be observed closely without binoculars. Mosquitoes and no-see-ums were pesty on this portion of the trail when I visited.

Many places along the trail offer access to the water. The Atlantic is so shallow and clear here that it's difficult to resist wading. Be prepared to share the flats with great egrets and blue herons and to get mud between your toes. The bottom is hard close to shore but becomes increasingly mushy the farther out you venture.

A huge brown pelican glided overhead when I rejoined the trail. The sounds of shorebirds, wind, and waves were a soothing symphony. Aromatic wildflowers grow along the sandy path, and land crabs burrow beside it. Although the mammals that reside here are limited because of the harsh environment, I did see a marsh hare scurry into the mangroves.

The Golden Orb Trail, named for the large, colorful spider

that spins webs so massive that small birds are sometimes caught in them, is not the only trail supervised by the park. The other is the Layton Trail, a lovely twenty-minute loop through a dense tropical hardwood hammock. This trail is not in the park proper, but on the Florida Bay side of US 1 about half a mile north of the

The pelican: "his beak holds as much as his belly can"

recreation area entrance. It provides a view of Long Key's rocky shoreline and Florida Bay.

Signs along the Layton Trail identify the interesting flora, which includes gumbo-limbo, pigeon plum, various cacti, wild coffee, Jamaica dogwood, seven-year apple, buttonwood, wild dilly, red mangrove, and wild lime. For a short distance, you will find yourself walking across rocks and dried sea grass a few steps in from the clear waters of Florida Bay. I saw a bonefish, one of Florida's most prized game fish, as it grubbed for crabs and shrimp in water less than a foot deep right against the shore. Having spent many unsuccessful hours in diligent pursuit of bonefish, I found it frustrating to be so near one with no fishing equipment.

Camping and swimming in the Atlantic are immensely popular in the park. The campground has sixty sites at the edge of the ocean, each with a table and grill and access to fresh water. About half the sites have electricity, and all are nestled beneath pine trees. A glorious breeze was blowing off the water when I visited.

It is possible to swim only a few feet behind your tent or trailer, but all swimming is unsupervised. The campground is quite busy, and reservations are taken up to sixty days in advance.

The waters surrounding the recreation area are renowned for wonderful fishing. You can often see fishing guides in skiffs stalking bonefish on the flats only a few hundred yards from the picnic area and campground. Bonefish, which feed in water so shallow that parts of their body are exposed, are caught only for sport and then released. Amazingly fast swimmers, they often peel off more than 100 yards of line in the first few seconds after being hooked.

Fishing opportunities in the area are limited without use of a boat. Rentals are available at Coconut Palma's at Mile Marker 59.8 in Grassy Key, Robbie's Marina at Mile Marker 77.5 in

Islamorada, or Bud n' Mary's Marina at Mile Marker 79.8, also in Islamorada.

Coconut Palmas (305-743-0552) rents sixteen- and eighteen-foot powerboats for $95.00 to $110.00 per day. Half-day rates range from $70.00 to $85.00. Bait, drinks, and tackle also are available.

Robbie's Marina (305-664-9814) has a fleet of rentals ranging from fourteen to twenty-seven feet. Costs are as little as $80.00 per day for a fourteen-footer to as much as $275.00 for a twenty-seven footer. Located on Florida Bay just south of the bridge at Lignumvitae Channel, Robbie's is a favorite stop of mine, whether I'm renting a vessel or not. Tarpon larger than six feet long and 100 pounds have schooled around the docks for years. For $1.00 per person, you can walk out on the dock and watch them. For $2.00 more, you get a bucket of fish to feed them.

Bud n' Mary's Marina (305-664-2461) has served local sportsmen since 1944. It has seventeen-foot boats available for $90.00 to $100.00 per day or $65.00 to $75.00 per half day. The dock also is home to a dozen offshore charter-fishing captains and twenty-five guides who specialize in capturing shallow-water species such as bonefish and tarpon. Rates on offshore boats, which are as large as fifty-five feet and carry as many as six passengers, run from $550.00 to $600.00 per day or $350.00 to $400.00 per half day. Skiff guides charge $300.00 per day or $200.00 per half day for two people and will take a third person for a small fee. Bait, diving equipment, drinks, and rod rentals also are available.

Fishing can be good from the bridge at Long Key Channel near the park. Anglers using live shrimp or cut mullet for bait catch mangrove snappers, small groupers, and grunts. The grunt is a bottom-dwelling species that doesn't have much of a reputation but is nonetheless excellent to eat. Large tarpon and barracuda are commonly seen from the bridge, but hooking them is not as easy.

The islands of Lignumvitae Key and Indian Key are convenient to Long Key State Recreation Area, although both are accessible only by boat. Regularly scheduled tours were available through the Long Key entrance station for years, but the park service was not offering them in the spring of 1993 and was unsure whether funding would be available in the future. Without a boat tour, the only other options for visitors are a private boat or rental.

Lignumvitae Key, one of the last remnants of a subtropical West Indies hammock, is a state botanical site a short distance offshore in Florida Bay. One-hour guided walks are given at 10:30 A.M., 1:00 P.M., and 2:30 P.M. Thursday through Monday. A fee of $1.00 per person is charged. The mosquitoes can be so bad here in late summer that tours are canceled. Long-sleeved shirts and long pants are suggested even though temperatures call

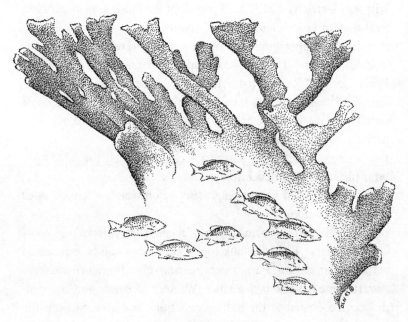

Coral reef off the Keys

for lighter clothing. Dark colors attract mosquitoes, so light-colored or white clothes are best. Mosquito netting for your face is a good idea.

Indian Key, a ten-acre state historic site in the Atlantic less than a mile from Lower Matecumbe Key, dates back to the time of prehistoric Indians. In the 1830s, it was designated the seat of Dade County. The foundations of buildings and cisterns dating back to the 1800s have been preserved by the park service.

Where: On US 1 at Mile Marker 67.5 in the Florida Keys.

Hours: 8:00 A.M. to sunset for day use. Only campers are allowed in after hours.

Admission: $3.75 for a driver and vehicle, fifty cents per person for each additional passenger up to eight, $1.50 per passenger over eight and for pedestrians, bicyclists, and members of organized tour groups. Camping is $23.59 per night for sites without electricity and $25.73 per night for those with electricity.

Best time to visit: October and November.

Activities: Ranger-guided programs are offered at 9:00 A.M. Wednesdays and Thursdays. Campfire programs are offered on Friday nights. Ranger-led activities include snorkeling in summer, bird watching in winter, and interpretive walks. The most popular recreations are camping, canoeing, fishing, hiking, picnicking, and swimming.

Concessions: Bicycles and canoes can be rented for $2.00 per hour plus a $10.00 deposit.

Pets: Not allowed in camping areas or on beaches. Guide dogs are always welcome.

Other: Calendars, Florida panther license plates, lapel pins, post cards, posters, T-shirts, tank tops, and videos can be purchased at the ranger station. Park brochures and other literature are free. A vertebrate list also is available. Weather forecasts and bug conditions are posted at the entrance station. Sea breezes keep the bugs tolerable most of the time, but they can be miserable in the summer if there is little wind.

For more information:
Long Key State Recreation Area, P.O. Box 776, Long Key,
FL 33001. 305-664-4815.

SANIBEL-CAPTIVA CONSERVATION FOUNDATION

I stumbled upon the Sanibel-Captiva Conservation Foundation
one Friday when I was disappointed to find the renowned Wildlife Drive at the Ding Darling National Wildlife Refuge closed. I
halfheartedly walked a few of the refuge's trails and then left,
feeling quite empty.

After only a few minutes' drive, I noticed a sign advertising
nature trails and turned into the driveway. What I found – an astounding preserve run by local citizens – saved the day.

The Sanibel-Captiva Conservation Foundation has quietly
conserved almost 1,100 acres of sensitive wetlands since the nonprofit organization was established in 1967. The freshwater
ecosystem here is unique because Sanibel and Captiva are barrier
islands surrounded by salt water. The freshwater Sanibel River
runs right through this preserve, one-fourth of which is covered
by seven hiking trails.

The property also includes a magnificent nature center with
exceptional interpretive exhibits, an education center with displays of seashells and carved birds, a native plant nursery, and a
wonderful gift shop. The walk that leads to the nature center is
lined with coco plum, gumbo-limbo, key lime, myrsine, paurotis
palm, seven-year apple, sea grape, strangler fig, wild coffee, and
wild olive trees. You will see many more of these trees on trails
accessible from the nature center.

Before you walk, visit the exhibits at the nature center.
These exhibits serve as a wonderful introduction to the area's
natural resources. Be sure to pick up a map detailing the trails,
along with an interpretive booklet describing animals and plants
and a bird list. All add greatly to the experience. Recent wildlife

sightings are posted inside next to the back door. The day I visited, the list included blue-winged teal, mottled ducks, robins, and a garter snake that allowed itself to be touched.

A short boardwalk with interpretive signs leads from the nature center to the trailhead. The boardwalk takes you across marsh grass, where you may see snowy egrets wading almost at your feet. The burrow of a gopher tortoise, a medium-size turtle that digs tunnels thirty feet long and twelve feet deep, is located at the end of the boardwalk on the right side.

Seven trails — none longer than three-quarters of a mile one way — converge at the end of the boardwalk. Visitors with limited time are encouraged to use the Elisha Camp Trail, a one-third-mile loop along a ridge and cordgrass swale. Other options include the longer East River and Sabal Palm trails. The former ends at an observation tower overlooking the Sanibel River. The latter goes to an abandoned alligator hole and past a grove with many air plants. Animals along the trails include alligators, anoles, bobcats, marsh hares, river otters, snakes, and tortoises. Great egrets, great blue and little blue herons, and ibis are among the common birds.

I chose the three-quarter-mile Sabal Palm Trail at the suggestion of staff member Cathy Boone and instantaneously felt the day's aggravation melt away. The trail is well canopied, so the temperature inside was a few degrees cooler than that outside — a welcome relief on an unusually warm spring day. Small anoles scurried across the path in front of me, and birds rustled in the trees. The lush landscape, almost all of which is labeled, includes wild cotton, Cherokee beans, Spanish needles, white indigo berries, guavas, snowberries, white stoppers, cat's-claws, blue porterweed, and saw palmettos. The saw palmetto produces a fruit that explorers said tastes like rotten cheese steeped in tobacco juice.

A while later, I stumbled across a gopher tortoise sitting at the edge of the sandy trail. The turtle, threatened because its preferred habitat is attractive to developers, tucked its head inside as I sauntered by. A few seconds later, it stuck its head back out and allowed me to take a series of photographs from only a few feet away.

The trail concludes at a watering hole dug by an alligator to ensure its water and food supply during a drought. Two ducks were paddling in Alligator Hole, but they retreated into cordgrass at the first sight of me. Close by, a pileated woodpecker was drilling holes in a palm tree.

I branched off onto other trails on the return trip and found them all as interesting as the first. One large southern black racer slithered almost between my feet, and another fled when I was a few feet away. Birds called back and forth in the trees above me, and I spotted several more tortoise burrows along the way.

Visitors to Sanibel and Captiva are lured primarily by the beaches and shells, and because of that, the islands have many condominiums and resorts. But almost half of the land area has been preserved by the federal government or state or local groups. This is one place you shouldn't miss.

Where: One mile west of the intersection of Tarpon Bay Road and Sanibel-Captiva Road on the way to Captiva Island. Take exit 21 from I-75. Go west on Daniels Road to Summerlin Road. Take left on Summerlin (going west to Sanibel Captiva island). Continue on Summerlin to Periwinkle Way. Turn right on Periwinkle to dead end at Tarpon Bay road. Turn right. At next stop sign turn left on Sanibel-Captiva road. The foundation is one mile on the left.

Hours: The nature center, trails, nature shop, and bookstore are open from 9:00 A.M. to 4:00 P.M. Monday through Saturday from November through May. The rest of the year, they are open from 9:00 A.M. to 3:00 P.M. Monday through Friday. The native plant nursery is open 9:00 A.M. to 5:00 P.M. Monday through Friday and 9:30 A.M. to 2:30 P.M. Saturday year-round.

Admission: $2.00 for adults and children age twelve and older.
Best time to visit: Birding is best in January and February, but
you can see birds year-round. The tourist traffic begins to slow
down after Easter. Biting insects are at their worst at the height of
summer.
Activities: One- to two-hour wetlands walks are held at 10:00
A.M. and 2:00 P.M. Monday through Saturday from November
30 to January 2. Walks are held at 10:00 A.M., 11:00 A.M., 1:00
P.M., and 2:00 P.M. Monday through Saturday from January 3
through April 15. One tour a day, at 8:30 A.M., is held on Monday, Tuesday, and Friday during the rest of the year. Other programs include beach walks, bird watching, boat tours, and
lectures. Days and hours vary, so call ahead for a schedule.
Concessions: None.
Pets: Not allowed.
Other: Sanibel Island is accessible only over a causeway, where
a toll of $1.50 per axle ($3.00 for cars) is charged. The nature
center and trails are accessible to people who are physically
challenged, and a wheelchair is available. Neither pets nor bicycles are allowed on the trails. The gift shop carries an extensive
selection of literature, birdhouses, bird feeders, and other nature-
oriented items. The nursery undertakes research, propagation,
and growth of native plants and also sells them.
For more information:
    Sanibel-Captiva Conservation Foundation, P.O. Box 839,
Sanibel, FL 33957. 813-472-2329.

BAHIA HONDA STATE PARK

Bahia Honda is Florida's southernmost state park. That geographic distinction is responsible for a natural environment
unique to the continental United States.
    The park contains sand dunes, mangrove forests, tropical

hardwood hammocks, and marine estuaries. But the 3.5 miles of white-sand beach is what makes this place wildly popular. Although the Keys are surrounded by water, they have few traditional beaches where you can walk or swim. Bahia Honda is the exception.

Various publications have ranked the beach among the country's ten best, and it's easy to understand why. Here you can still find solitude and beauty, and the skyline is not marred by unsightly condominiums and skyscraper hotels.

The park sits on a narrow strip of land bordered by the Gulf of Mexico on one side and the Atlantic Ocean on the other. The property contains the old Bahia Honda Bridge, the most scenic span on the Overseas Railroad that once linked the Keys to the mainland and Miami. A walk on the old bridge offers a stunning view of the mangrove islands that dot the surrounding water, which takes on hues ranging from white and light green to aqua and powder blue.

The beach along the road, only a short distance from the entrance gate, is wonderful for wading at low tide. People plant chairs on sugar-white sandbars and while away the day. A suitable beach for combing and swimming stretches all the way from the southernmost tip of the park to Sandspur Beach to the north. Throughout the area, the beach is protected from the road by dunes ten to twenty feet tall. Waves crash and gulls cry as you walk along the shore.

Many types of recreation are offered within the park, almost all beach or water oriented. With the exception of birds, the animal life is fairly limited because of the habitat.

A vertebrate list provided by the park includes ninety-three birds, forty of which are either abundant or seasonally common. When I visited in May, guests were asked to be careful not to disturb the nests of least terns, a threatened species that lays its eggs in gravel or directly on the beach. Rangers told me that wading birds and shorebirds are common, as are winter sightings of broad-winged hawks and summer sightings of magnificent frigate birds. I noticed an osprey constructing a nest atop a raised platform along the road between the ranger station and the concession area and saw palm warblers close to a path that leads from the concession area to the scenic bridge.

The only mammals known to be present in the park or its adjacent waters are raccoons, evening bats, endangered manatees, and bottle-nosed dolphins. The raccoons are bothersome in the campground, and guests are warned not to leave food unattended or to bring any food or water into their tents.

Endangered Atlantic loggerhead turtles crawl ashore to lay eggs at night starting in May. Nesting lasts a few months, and rangers monitor the activity closely. No turtle-watching programs are offered, and visitors are expected to keep their distance if they are lucky enough to stumble upon a sea turtle.

The recreation area contains three tent and trailer campgrounds with a total of eighty sites. The twenty-four sites in the popular Sandspur Camping Area are well spaced, shady, and deep and are only a short distance from the beach. Reservations are accepted up to sixty days in advance and are suggested. Campgrounds are full almost every night in the winter, and it's not unusual to be on a waiting list for three to five days if you don't make reservations.

The park also has six cabins accessible by boat at the edge of the Gulf of Mexico. Reservations are taken up to a year in advance and are necessary throughout the year. Cabins sleep up to eight people and come with central air-conditioning and heat. They are equipped with basic cooking and eating utensils, linens, and towels and have decks with a picnic table, grill, and outside shower. Stays are limited to two to seven days.

Picnicking is popular at shaded tables beside the water near the old bridge and at Sandspur Beach. Benches near the old bridge overlook a protected swimming area with a sandy beach. A few have grills, and all are close to trash cans and recycling bins.

A series of pavilions at Sandspur Beach is set back only a few yards from the ocean. Boardwalks lead over sensitive sand dunes to the water. Bathhouses and showers are convenient to the pavilions.

The Silver Palm Trail, only about one-half mile round-trip, starts at the far end of the parking area at Sandspur Beach. The trail has a series of stations set up to correspond with a self-guided booklet, but the literature box was bare and rangers at the entrance station had no copies of the booklet when I visited. Palms, pigeon plums, poisonwood, sea grapes, seven-year apples, and white stoppers are all visible along the trail.

The waters adjacent to Bahia Honda provide spectacular tarpon fishing. This acrobatic silvery game fish, actually a member of the sardine family, is caught around the old and new bridges using live crabs and mullet for bait. It is possible – but not probable – to catch one from the bridge or shore. A skiff is necessary to pursue bigger tarpon once they are hooked. Anglers are expected to release any tarpon they catch. A special permit is necessary to keep them.

Fishing is not allowed from the new bridge across Bahia Honda Channel and is difficult from the old bridge because it is so high. Fishermen hook small groupers, grunts, several species of snapper, and even cobias from the breakwater at the end of the swimming area close to the old bridge. Those with access to a boat do well bottom fishing between the bridges and close to the pilings and occasionally even hook barracuda and huge sharks. Guides specializing in tarpon fishing at Bahia Honda Channel can be contacted through the Marathon Chamber of Commerce (305-743-5417) or the Lower Keys Chamber of Commerce in Big Pine Key (305-872-2411).

Where: Twelve miles south of Marathon on US 1 at Mile Marker 37 on Bahia Honda Key.
Hours: Day use is from 8:00 A.M. to sunset. Only campers are allowed inside after dark.

Admission: The day-use fee is $3.75 for the driver and vehicle and fifty cents per passenger up to eight. The fee is $1.50 per passenger over eight and for bicyclists and pedestrians. Children under six are free. Camping fees range from $23.59 per night for an inland site without electricity to $27.95 for a waterfront site with a full hookup. Furnished cabins rent for $96.85 per night from September 15 to December 14 and for $124.60 per night from December 15 to September 14.

Best time to visit: March and April. The worst time to visit is June through August, when its hot, humid, and buggy.

Activities: The most popular activities are walking the beach, boating, picnicking, and swimming.

Concessions: Bicycles can be rented for $2.14 per hour, $6.42 per half day, or $9.63 per day. Kayaks are available for $10.70 per half day and $26.75 per day. Snorkeling equipment costs $7.49 per day, with a $50.00 deposit required. The set includes a mask, snorkel, and fins and is fine for swimming off the beach. Dive flags ($4.28 per day) are mandatory for snorkelers who venture out beyond the boundaries of two marked swimming areas. Snorkeling trips to the Looe Key National Marine Sanctuary depart from the parks marina at 9:30 A.M. and 2:00 P.M. in the summer and 9:00 A.M. and 1:30 P.M. in the winter. The cost is $23.54 per person, with $5.35 charged for equipment rental. A marina with nineteen slips accepts vessels with a draft of four feet or more for eighty-five cents per foot per night. Slips come with electricity and water.

Pets: Not allowed on the beaches, in the cabins or campground, in the pavilions or picnic areas, or in the water. Elsewhere, they are permitted only on a six-foot, hand-held leash. Guide dogs are always welcome.

Other: Bait and tackle, beach equipment, cameras and film, diving and snorkeling gear, ice cream, jewelry, limited groceries, reading material , snacks, stamps, and videotapes are available at the concession building from 8:00 A.M. to 5:00 P.M. Minimal park literature was available when I visited in May 1993.

For more information:
Bahia Honda State Park, Route 1, Box 782, Big Pine Key,
FL 33043. 305-872-2353.

MUSEUM OF NATURAL HISTORY
OF THE FLORIDA KEYS

The Museum of Natural History of the Florida Keys is note-
worthy for many reasons. It is a fine example of what a group of
private citizens can accomplish on a local level against long
odds. The museum is located on a 63.5-acre property known as
Crane Point Hammock, a tropical forest that is home to 160
native and 50 exotic plant species, including 10 that are endangered. The property also contains prehistoric and pre-Columbian
Indian sites and the remnants of an eighteenth-century Bahamian
village.

The Florida Keys Land & Sea Trust, a nonprofit organization dedicated to preserving sensitive areas, purchased Crane
Point Hammock in 1989 and saved it from almost certain development. A strip shopping center is located directly across the
highway, and myriad shops and fast-food restaurants dot the surrounding area.

The museum, opened in 1990, has surprisingly good exhibits for such a small place. On display are shell tools, pottery,
and other relics from ancient Indians; artifacts from ships that
were wrecked hundreds of years ago; dioramas depicting local
wildlife; and a wonderful walk-through exhibit of an artist's ren-
dering of an underwater cave. The latter display is three stories
tall. Replicas of species such as the barracuda, dolphin, grouper,
marlin, mutton snapper, and shark are placed appropriately in the
water table.

A short boardwalk leads from the main museum building to
the adjacent Florida Keys Children's Museum, which is just as
interesting to parents as it is to kids. The boardwalk crosses a

saltwater tidal lagoon stocked with many native saltwater fish, including moray eels, lemon and nurse sharks, and stingrays. Angelfish, blue runners, cowfish, filefish, mangrove snappers, mullet, scorpion fish, sheepsheads, parrot fish, permits, porkfish, puffers, and rock beauties also are present. The fish in the lagoon are most active during the 11:00 A.M. feeding.

Exhibits in the children's museum include a replica of a Spanish galleon where kids can dress up like pirates, a science center with a microscope, a mock railway station, aquariums, marine touch tanks, and a special display of plants and animals that should never be touched. The latter includes the potentially fatal manchineel, poisonwood, fire coral, a Portuguese man-of-war, a scorpion, and a coral snake.

The touch tanks contain objects safe for humans to handle. Creatures include hermit and horseshoe crabs, sand dollars, sea anemones, shovel-nosed lobsters, and sea urchins.

Another nearby tank contains the clawless Florida spiny lobster, which propels itself backward to elude divers and predators. Regulations allow for the tasty crustacean to be harvested only at certain times of the year, and these regulations are strictly enforced. Unlike their northern relatives, spiny lobsters are harmless and rely on their hard, spiny shells to deter enemies. Divers have likened them to a rose bush, so care must be taken.

The same aquarium includes blue, spider, and stone crabs. Stone crabs are one of Florida's most important commercial species. Stone crab claws are delicious when served with a mustard sauce or drawn butter. Unlike other crabs, the entire animal isn't harvested. Only one claw is taken so that the crustaceans can fend for themselves while a new claw grows back.

Conchs, snail-like creatures that live underwater in large shells, are on display in another exhibit. Once harvested to near extinction in the Keys, they are now protected and grow in the wild and as part of aquaculture projects. Their tasty meat is used primarily in chowders, fritters, and salads.

The property's well-manicured grounds also contain a one-quarter-mile loop trail. Markers correspond with descriptions in a pamphlet that can be borrowed from the gift shop. About a third of the tree species native to the hammock can be seen along the trail, which will be enlarged in the future to include the former Bahamian village. Trees include the black-bead, black ironwood, blolly, buttonwood, coconut palm, darling plum, gumbo-limbo, inkwood, Jamaica dogwood, pigeon plum, poisonwood, red mangrove, saffron plum, Spanish stopper, strangler fig, thatch palm, and wild dilly.

The Spanish stopper is a small evergreen that produces fruit eaten by birds. Its roots have a bay rum scent and are used in making cologne.

Indians used the leaves of the thatch palm to construct homes. The trees, now officially threatened, dominate the scenery along the trail, with their huge fronds shading the forest floor. Though common here, this species is becoming increasingly rare elsewhere.

Poisonwood, related to poison ivy and poison sumac, is protected in this part of the Keys because its fruit is critical to the survival of the endangered white-crowned pigeon. The pigeon is found in Crane Point Hammock year-round. Bird-watchers come to see these birds and wild canaries from Cuba, which visit the hammock each spring. Other birds commonly seen at Crane Point and in the Marathon area in general include American kestrels, burrowing owls, herons, egrets, ospreys, pelicans, and a variety of warblers.

Lignum vitae, an extremely hard wood with very small green leaves, can be seen outside the museum's front door. The tree's wood is so hard that it is used to make ball bearings in nuclear submarines. The lignum vitae produces a small purple flower in the spring.

OTHER ECOLOGICAL ATTRACTIONS

The Museum of Natural History of the Florida Keys is just one of a handful of places of unusual environmental interest in the Marathon area. Other places to see include the Dolphin Research Center at Mile Marker 59 on Grassy Key, the Hidden Harbor Marine Research Institute at Mile Marker 48.5 in Marathon, the Seven Mile Bridge, which begins at the west end of Marathon, and the National Key Deer Wildlife Refuge near Mile Marker 31 on Big Pine Key.

The DOLPHIN RESEARCH CENTER (305-289-0002 or 289-1121) is a nonprofit educational facility that offers walking tours, swim-with-dolphin programs, and workshops. Costs range from $7.50 for educational walking tours to $80.00 for in-water encounter programs. Walking tours are given to the general public at 10:00 A.M., 12:30 P.M., 2:00 P.M., and 3:30 P.M. Wednesday through Sunday. Reservations for encounter programs are accepted on the first day of the month for the following month. That means anyone who wishes to come in March should call on the first day of February, and so on. The program is so popular that reservations are usually filled within two days.

The HIDDEN HARBOR MARINE RESEARCH INSTITUTE is on the property of the Hidden Harbor Motel. It is the brainchild of motel owner/environmentalist Richie Moretti and Marathon fishing guide Tina Brown. The couple converted the motel's saltwater tidal pool into a giant aquarium and stocked it with fish caught on Tina's charters. Among the fish are one-hundred-plus pound tarpon, fat groupers, permits, redfish, snappers, and snook. The area around the tidal pool is enclosed, but it is possible to see through the screen. Tanks containing endangered sea turtles sit at one corner of the pool. Moretti and Brown, who have been featured on national television and in *National Geographic* magazine, are funding a sea turtle study and doing much of the work with the help of biologists and a local veterinarian. They are investigating the cause of tumors that infect a majority of all sea turtles and kill many of them. Until they took up the cause, little research on the topic had been done on the state or federal level. Moretti also purchased a lounge on property adjacent to the motel and converted it into a hospital that specializes in treating sea turtles and marine mammals. Tours of the facilities and educational programs can be arranged by calling the motel office at 305-743-5321.

The old SEVEN MILE BRIDGE, one of the original structures on an Overseas Railroad that once stretched from Homestead to Key West, is now open to bikers, hikers, and fishermen. The view of the Atlantic Ocean and Florida Bay is spectacular, and at times you may see free-swimming dolphins, huge tarpon, barracuda, and sharks from the bridge. The bridge serves as a perfect fishing pier. Species caught include cobias, grunts, groupers, mangrove and mutton snappers, sharks, and snook.

The NATIONAL KEY DEER WILDLIFE REFUGE (305-872-2239) is home to a vast majority of the remaining 300-odd key deer, a tiny subspecies of the Virginia white-tailed deer. The animals are gravely imperiled by development, and forty or more are killed every year by cars. The refuge is worth a visit for many reasons, but mainly because the people who run it have done a splendid job in the face of great pressure from builders, local landowners, and bureaucrats interested in development. It contains walking trails and a fresh-water pond. Deer are commonly seen, especially in the early morning and late afternoon. Feeding the deer is prohibited because it encourages unnatural behavior and often causes them to cross busy roads.

Where: Located on US 1 at Mile Marker 50 in Marathon.

Hours: 9:00 A.M. to 5:00 P.M. Monday through Saturday and noon to 5:00 P.M. Sunday.

Admission: $5.00 for adults, $4.00 for seniors, and $2.00 for students.

Best time to visit: Anytime.

Activities: The fish in the lagoon are fed daily at 11:00 A.M. Inquire about occasional wildlife programs, concerts, and slide shows. Special tours can be arranged in advance, and the entire property can be rented for birthdays and special events.

Concessions: None.

Pets: Not allowed. Guide dogs are always welcome.

Other: The bookstore/gift shop has a wonderful selection of materials, including children's literature, field guides, jewelry,

pottery, paintings, and wood carvings. A superb children's reading room and library is open to the public during visiting hours.
For more information:
Museum of Natural History of the Florida Keys, 5550 Overseas Highway, Marathon, FL 33050. 305-743-9100.

BISCAYNE NATIONAL PARK

Biscayne National Park was ground zero for Hurricane Andrew. The storm came on shore directly over barrier islands within the park and moved through the visitors center before continuing on through Homestead. Visiting the park underscores the ferocity of the storm. Even nine months later, the area looked as though Andrew had just blown through.

This park is 95 percent water, but the remaining 5 percent received heavy damage. Several mangrove islands in the bay were almost totally destroyed. The wind peeled the bark off nearly every branch. The small fraction of mangroves that survived did so because they were submerged by the tidal surge. Two of three buildings housing rangers on Elliot Key also were leveled. The islands, formerly open for picnicking, are now closed to the public until further notice.

Park headquarters, located on the mainland at Convoy Point, has been rebuilt better than before. An interpretive display, bookstore, and theater opened to the public the week I visited. Rangers are available to answer questions and will start an informative slide show on request. The slide show gives the history of the region and the park, taking the visitor through the years of Indian battles, pineapple plantations, and the ever-vigilant and futile fight against the mosquitoes. An amateur video of Hurricane Andrew also is shown upon request. The video is special to the rangers not only because it documents the preparation for, destruction of, and recovery from the storm but also because it is dedicated to the memory of ranger Natividad "Tito" Rohena, who died in the hurricane.

Take the boat ride to the reef. Captain Ed Davidson has been running the charter for years, and his storytelling ability is second to none. He and his mates know the history of the region and can identify the thousands of fish and coral visible from the glass-bottom boat. On the way out to the reef, you will pass Boca Chita Key, Sands Key, Elliot Key, Adams Key, and Caesar Creek. Caesar Creek is named after an early Florida pirate named Black Caesar, who used to lie in wait in that canal hoping for an unsuspecting sailboat to come by.

Now there is another legend to add to the lore of Caesar Creek. During Hurricane Andrew, three men decided to ride out the storm aboard the *Leviathan*, a forty-eight-foot sport boat. The boat was uninsured, and the men thought that Caesar Creek would provide shelter from the storm. During the hurricane, one man was swept overboard, never to be found again. Another was killed instantly when a two-by-six flew through the cabin wall, decapitating him and breaking through the cabin door behind him. His body was washed overboard when the boat was knocked over and blown into the mangroves, cutting a swath behind it. His body was found five days later. The third man survived by riding out the storm huddled in a coffinlike bait well that had been constructed around the tuna tower. The nightmare is recounted in the hurricane video shown at the visitors center.

The ride also takes you past the former ranger quarters and docks on Elliot Key. Reconstruction hadn't yet begun and plans for the islands were up in the air at the time of my visit.

At the reef, the undersea world looks tranquil and magical. Brightly colored parrot fish abound. Staghorn coral, brain coral, and soft sea fans stand ready to provide shelter for tangs, sergeant majors, lobsters, and angelfish. A slimy green moray eel nervously peeked out of its home as the boat traveled slowly across the reef.

The sea has a wonderful way of healing, and a visit to Biscayne National Park has great restorative powers. Take either the three-hour boat tour or the longer snorkeling trip. The reef is as spectacular as John Pennekamp Coral Reef State Park, found at the south end of the reef off Key Largo, but the absence of crowds and the personalized tours make for a more enjoyable trip.

Where: Approximately seven miles east of Florida's Turnpike. Take the Tallahassee Road exit off the turnpike and follow signs. From the Keys, take US 1 north through Homestead to S.W. 328th Street and turn right. Follow it to the park.

Hours: 8:00 A.M. to sunset daily.

Admission: Free.

Best time to visit: Winter for a boat trip; summer for snorkeling.

Activities: Glass-bottom boat rides and snorkeling trips are offered by an independent concessionaire.

Concessions: Captain Ed Davidson has been running the glass-bottom boat and snorkeling concession at the park for years. In fact, when people think of Biscayne National Park, they immediately think of Captain Ed. As of May 1993, the glass-bottom boat ride was offered daily from 10:00 A.M. to 1:00 P.M. The cost is $16.50 for adults and $8.50 for children ages one through twelve. Children under one are free. A snorkeling trip is offered daily from 1:30 P.M. to 5:30 P.M. The cost is $24.50 per person including mask, fins, snorkel, and vest. Scuba diving is available for $34.50 per person plus equipment rental. Reservations are required. It is very important to call to confirm the schedule on the morning of your trip. On days where attendance is very low, trips may be canceled. Call 305-247-2400 for information and reservations.

Pets: Not permitted.

Other: A visitors center on the mainland has a wonderful interpretive center with displays, a bookstore, and a small theater for films and slide shows.

For more information:
Biscayne National Park, P.O. Box 1369, Homestead, FL 33090. 305-247-7275.

DRY TORTUGAS NATIONAL PARK

My husband and I have been to Dry Tortugas National Park twice. The first time was before we were married, and my husband was still trying to convince me to marry him. His ploy was to whisk me off to a deserted island, camp for the Fourth of July weekend with friends on their forty-five-foot custom-designed motorboat, and then fly back to Key West aboard a seaplane. It worked. The trip was magical – almost as wonderful as when we repeated it four years later.

Fort Jefferson is located several hours by boat from the nearest convenience store, hotel, or bait shop. Because it is so far off the beaten path, it still offers adventures for the willing.

Our trip to Fort Jefferson began in Marathon. We loaded up the boat with supplies and then made our way under the Seven Mile Bridge to the Atlantic side of the Keys. It is safer to travel there through the open water of the Atlantic than to navigate through the channels and flats of the Gulf Keys. Even when navigating through the Atlantic, it is important to have an accurate nautical chart.

Five hours later – and three hours after we saw the last of Key West – we spotted the fort on the horizon. The remnants of the brick fortress tower above the palms on the deserted island, the only one visible. On the approach to the park, the channel leads past a rift where thousands of birds rest before taking flight again.

It was a busy weekend for the park. We were one of four boats anchoring in the designated mooring area. As the sun set, we sat on the bow, drinking wine and watching the sky change from orange and gold to pink and mauve to violet and indigo to black and gold.

We ate dinner and talked under the stars until bedtime. Even after our hosts had retired to their room, we sat above deck and stared at the stars. I have never seen so many stars so clearly. They have never seemed so close. The only other light was from the citronella candle on our bow.

The next morning, we left the boat moored to its anchor and packed a motorized inflatable with barbecue supplies and plenty of water then headed for the fort. Construction of the fort began in 1846 and continued for decades. It was never really finished. The centerpiece is a six-sided, half-mile-around stone and brick fortress with walls more than eight feet thick. The fort is uninhabited, but rangers spend the nights on a nearby island with housing facilities.

The fort was originally designed to aid the United States' control of the Gulf of Mexico and the Caribbean. Though it was never finished, the Union forces were garrisoned here during the Civil War. After several years and several thousand dollars, the Army discovered that there is no fresh water on the island. The only fresh water available is from rainwater or desalinization.

After the war, the fort was used as a prison, principally for Dr. Samuel Mudd, the doctor found guilty of treason for treating Abraham Lincoln's assassin, John Wilkes Booth. Mudd served many years in solitary confinement in a dark and dank cell until one by one, his captors fell ill from yellow fever. Dr. Mudd treated the sick and was awarded his freedom.

Through the years, weather has taken its toll on the building. Vegetation has overtaken the top battlements, even though the surrounding area is a desert and scrub habitat. Bricks have loosened, crumbled, and blown away. Several staircases are blocked off for safety. In some areas, entire side walls are missing.

We explored the caverns of the fort, looked through the

battlements to the moat below, climbed on top of the walls to take in the breathtaking views, and then made our way back to the beach for a barbecue. Later, we explored the deserted beaches of nearby Loggerhead Key, inspecting shells and hoping to find a gold doubloon that had washed up from one of the many sunken ships in the area.

After a long, relaxing walk, we returned to the boat for stern showers — a soaping and a quick rinse with the boat's fresh-water hose. After catching several snappers for dinner, we continued to fish for fun. We caught barracuda, blue runners, strawberry and Nassau groupers, and mackerel. One of us nabbed a trophy mackerel, only to have a ten-foot shark come up and bite it off just below the head.

We spent the next day snorkeling just off the island, about twenty-five feet from our boat — the same place that had been visited by a shark just slightly less than twice my size. Luckily, it did not return, but when we realized our folly, we stayed closer to shore.

We could see beautiful brain coral with patches of fire coral, purple sea fans, and colorful pink coral along the sea bottom. Blue tangs, sergeant majors, angelfish, barracuda, mutton snappers, and six-foot-long tarpon swam close by. The water was warm and delightful.

The next morning, we flew back to Key West. The pilot kept the plane's windows open, and the warm air blew in our faces. From far above the water, we were able to see shipwrecks, solitary islands topped with magnificent estates, and schools of dolphins swimming below.

Where: A tiny cluster of island approximately sixty miles due west of Key West in the Gulf of Mexico.
Hours: Sunrise to sunset daily.
Admission: Free.
Best time to visit: November through July. Visiting during the

most active months of hurricane season, typically the end of August through September, requires much planning and the ability to maintain constant contact with a news source. There are no safe harbors in the Dry Tortugas.

Activities: Exploring the ruins of a historic fort, very primitive beach camping, swimming, snorkeling, fishing, bird watching, boating, and sailing.

Concessions: None. Bring enough food and drink to last the visit. Bring lots of water, ice, and Gatorade, especially in the summer.

Pets: Not permitted.

Other: Seaplane trips are offered on weekends from Marathon Key and Key West. Call Chalks International Airlines in Fort Lauderdale at 305-359-7980, in Miami at 305-371-8628, and in Key West at 305-292-3637; Key West Seaplane Service, 305-294-6978; or Aerojet, 305-772-5070. Contact the park for other charter possibilities.

For more information:

Dry Tortugas National Park, P.O. Box 6208, Key West, FL 33041. 305-247-7700.

5
The Everglades

EVERGLADES NATIONAL PARK

First-time visitors to Everglades National Park often feel as exasperated as they do fulfilled. They enter one of the world's most famous environmental preserves expecting to be dazzled but end up wondering why there has been such a fuss. There are no mountains, as at Denali National Park. There are no gorges, as in the Grand Canyon. And there are no dramatic cliffs at ocean's edge, as at Acadia. What there is, as far as the eye can see, is grass. So much that it nearly stretches from coast to coast. So much that, initially, everything looks the same.

Of course, Everglades National Park has much more to offer than first meets the eye. It encompasses such a complex ecosystem, with such diverse habitats and plant and animal life, that it confounds the mind. It has mangroves and marshes, pinelands and prairies, and bays, ponds, and sloughs. But appreciating the vastness and versatility of this resource, takes a little time. Its beauty and importance elude those who never leave their automobiles or venture off the beaten path.

Everglades National Park, comprising more than 1.5 million acres, begs for exploration, and its mysteries are best unraveled by adventurous souls. True appreciation comes with understanding, which is why I suggest taking part in ranger-guided programs out of the Royal Palm and Flamingo visitor centers, Shark Valley, and the Gulf Coast Ranger Station. All but a handful of the tours are free and more educational than those offered in the park for a fee by private concessionaires. Schedules for both ranger-led and commercial activities are available at the visitors centers and are printed in handouts received upon entering the park.

Intimidation is the biggest obstacle that must be overcome to enjoy a trip here. The park is so massive that newcomers are at a loss as to how or where to begin. Don't try to do too much. It takes a while for your eyes to adjust to the raw beauty of the Everglades and to focus on the hidden birds and protected plants in the vast plains.

Plan to spend at least three to five days inside the main park entrance west of Homestead and at least two days each at Shark Valley and the Gulf Coast. Treat each as a separate destination, and don't try to visit all in a few days. Each trip requires driving a considerable distance: fifty miles from the main gate west of Homestead to Shark Valley, ninety-two miles from the main gate to the Gulf Coast Ranger Station between Chokoloskee and Everglades City.

The best approach to visiting any of the three locations is to wade right in. The more actively and aggressively you explore the park, the more rewarding the experience will be. Everglades is the only national park in this hemisphere designated a World Heritage Site and Wetland of International Importance. Its magnificence becomes clear with effort and patience.

The best time to visit the park is in the winter. Oppressive heat and ravenous mosquitoes make summer visits inadvisable.

WHERE TO BEGIN

Begin your exploration of Everglade National Park with an eye-opening drive to the main entrance nine miles west of US 1 in Homestead. The road that leads directly to the guardhouse, State 9336, winds through the area gutted by Hurricane Andrew on August 24, 1992. The storm's 200 mph gusts destroyed row upon row of houses, snapped off concrete power poles at the ground, reduced some mobile homes to shrapnel, and twisted other mobile homes around fence posts. Rebuilding Homestead and the neighboring community of Florida City will take many years.

Andrew's eye passed directly over the park headquarters, wrecking boardwalks and buildings and snapping off trees like matchsticks for the first twenty miles along the main road. The damage was most severe in the vicinity of the entrance and led to a four-month park closure.

Hurricanes have shaped the Everglades' ecosystem for millions of years. Despite causing much destruction, Andrew unleashed a fury of regrowth and reproduction, offering the inquisitive eye much to see. Currently, inconveniences as a result of the storm are few and have little effect on the quality of a visit.

The first stop in Everglades National Park is the main visitors center, a few hundred yards from the main gate, where one-week admission fees are collected. The cost is $5.00 for cars and $3.00 for bicyclists. Passengers in cars are admitted free.

Park brochures and activity schedules are available at the main visitors center – now a trailer – a few hundred yards past the entrance. The trailer will be used for about three years while a new permanent facility is being built. The previous structure was razed after being battered by Andrew.

The Royal Palm Visitor Center, four miles past the main entrance, is the next stop for many visitors. It contains two of the park's most popular trails and is the site of numerous ranger-led programs.

Royal Palm is a wonderful place to begin your exploration because it offers a marvelous sampling of Everglades flora and fauna. Alligators sun themselves on the banks of the canal beside the Anhinga Trail, a half-mile tour through a freshwater river via a wheelchair-accessible paved surface and boardwalk. The trail is named after the anhinga, a large, slender diving bird with a long, skinny neck. After swimming underwater to catch their prey, the birds roost in trees with their wings spread out in the sun.

Wading birds such as the great blue heron stand like statues at the water's edge, waiting for just the right moment to spear unsuspecting prey with their pointy bills. Their dinner list includes fish and insects — and occasionally something much larger. Visitors were recently treated to a rare tug-of-war between a heron and a water snake. The big bird won the battle, but not before the snake wrapped itself around the heron's neck in a last-ditch effort to keep from being consumed.

Hawks, ospreys, and vultures circle overhead. If you're lucky, an osprey will dive to the surface of the water and fly off clutching a wriggling fish in its razor-sharp talons. Migrating birds from the North also make Everglades National Park their home in the cool winter months.

Mayan cichlids and oscars, prolific nonnative fish, swim a few inches beneath the water's surface in hopes that the fruit of a strangler fig tree will fall at the water's edge. Ask a ranger to demonstrate this phenomenon by picking a few figs if they are in season. The fish eat them and help propagate the trees by purging what they have consumed. The seeds, swept by the wind and tide, eventually coming to rest on a bank and grow if they find fertile soil.

Plump largemouth bass can be seen fanning their beds in crystal-clear water a few feet deep. Other species include bluegills, sunfish, and Florida gars, but fishing is prohibited.

A rare Florida cougar

The activity around the slough, a wide, shallow river that flows through a saw grass prairie, is most intense at dusk. In the course of a few minutes, you'll see alligators, turtles, and dozens of species of wading and diving birds — including anhingas; cormorants; gallinules; little blue, great blue, greenbacked, and tricolored herons; ibis; and snowy egrets — before they hunker down for the night.

Once you have familiarized yourself with the slough, return to the Royal Palm Visitor Center and seek out the adjacent Gumbo Limbo Trail. There you will be introduced to yet another Everglades habitat, the tropical hardwood hammock. This half-mile walk is most productive if done in the company of a ranger. An afternoon walk is scheduled daily in the winter at 3:30 P.M.

Twice I have taken Gumbo Limbo walks with ranger Frank Aranzamendi, and both were a pleasure. The tours lasted well beyond the advertised fifty minutes, mostly due to Aranzamendi's attention to detail and willingness to answer each and every question.

The trail, named after the only softwood tree in the hammock, passes through a junglelike environment that was so dense before Hurricane Andrew that it resulted in a temperature drop of seven degrees. Now, cracked, split, and toppled trees are everywhere. Sunlight penetrates where a tree-to-tree ceiling once covered the trail.

"The first day I was in here after the hurricane, it was naked," Aranzamendi says. "It looked like somebody went through with a blowtorch. But regrowth has been tremendous. This is the beginning of a new cycle. It will be back to the way I remember it in ten to fifteen years."

Those who have never been on the Gumbo Limbo Trail will still be impressed by its lushness. Those who visited it before Andrew will be amazed by nature's pruning.

Aranzamendi takes time to stop and talk about each type of tree found along the trail. There are far too many to mention, but the list includes gumbo-limbo, poisonwood, white stopper, pigeon plum, wild coffee, royal palm, live oak, strangler fig, and mahogany trees.

Morning glories grow in the soil beside the trail. Ferns cling to limbs and trunks in every direction. Wild orchids — thirty-six different kinds — poke out of crevices and grow in the tops of trees.

Aranzamendi's informative patter arouses the curiosity and stimulates the imagination. He tells us that the gumbo-limbo is sometimes referred to as the "tourist tree" because its bark gets red and peels just like an unwary sunbather who gets burned at the beach. He notes that the first carousel horses were carved from gumbo-limbo and that fishermen once used it to make floats for their nets. He also relates that crushed gumbo-limbo bark is an antidote for poisonwood, a look-alike tree that can cause a serious rash when brushed against.

Aranzamendi goes on to explain how settlers boiled the leaves of the white stopper, a tall shrub, and drank the brew to stop dysentery. And he tells us that all types of downed trees provide a new home for woodpeckers and that bobcats, lizards, opossums, owls, endangered panthers, raccoons, red-shouldered

Flamingoes

and short-tailed hawks, and lingus tree snails rely on the hammock for food and refuge.

Other popular ranger-led programs regularly scheduled out of Royal Palm include 2.5-hour slogs through cypress trees, sawgrass, and water; pinelands trail walks; mahogany hammock tours; and wildlife identification walks around the Anhinga Trail.

Guided bird-watching tours, car caravans, canoe trips, slide shows, talks, and walks are offered regularly out of the Royal Palm and Flamingo visitor centers, both accessible

---

ACTIVITIES AT FLAMINGO

The following is a sample of winter ranger-led activities at the Flamingo Visitor Center. The schedule was used from February through March 6, 1993.

• Early Bird Special, 7:30 A.M. Thursday and Saturday. Join a ranger for an easy ninety-minute stroll. Check at the Flamingo Visitor Center for the location.

• Glades by Canoe, 8:30 A.M., Sunday, Tuesday, and Wednesday. Leave the road behind and paddle into the Everglades. Reservations required, in person, no earlier than one day before the trip, at the Flamingo Visitor Center.

• Discover the Everglades, 10:00 A.M. Monday, Tuesday, and Thursday. A 1.5- to 2.5-hour activity to explore plants, marine creatures, or wading-bird behavior. May involve walking. Check at the Flamingo Visitor Center for details.

• Everglades Adventure, 2:00 P.M. Sunday, Tuesday, Friday, and Saturday. Enjoy a two- to four-hour hike, bike, or wet walk into a freshwater marsh or salty bayshore. Check at the Flamingo Visitor Center for details.

• Naturalist Knapsack, 4:00 P.M. Sunday, Monday, Wednesday, Thursday, and Saturday. A thirty-minute talk at the Flamingo Visitor Center.

• Evening Program, 7:30 P.M. daily. Find out what makes the Everglades like no other place on earth. Flamingo campground amphitheater, one hour.

---

through the main gate west of Homestead. Daily schedules are posted at the main visitors center just inside the park entrance, four miles away at Royal Palm, and thirty-eight miles farther along at Flamingo.

Numerous boat and tram tours also are run out of the marina at Flamingo by a private concession company. Fees ranging from $7.30 to $29.50 per adult are charged. Schedules are posted at the main visitors center and at Flamingo. Bicycles, canoes, and skiffs also are available for rent at Flamingo.

The 1.6-mile Snake Bight Trail, a few miles from Flamingo, is one of the most popular trails in the park because it offers wonderful bird watching at the end of the path. I've seen thousands of wading birds – in every direction as far as the eye can see – from the boardwalk there. The problem is that the mosquitoes are terrible until you get out in the open at the end.

"If no other mosquitoes are biting anywhere in the continental United States, they will be at Snake Bight," ranger Stever Robinson says. Robinson suggests bringing or renting a bicycle for use on the trails. "When you are on a bike, the mosquitoes usually don't figure out that you are there until you are past them and gone."

ACCOMMODATIONS

The only accommodations within Everglades National Park can be found at the Flamingo Lodge, which offers motel rooms, cottages, and suites. Prices range from $52.00 per night for a room in the slow summer season (May 1 through October 31) to $89.00 per night in the busiest part of winter (December 15 through March 31). Cottages increase from $62.00 to $105.00 in the same period; suites go from $82.00 to $134.00. The rooms are comfortable and clean and almost always full in the winter.

The lodge's restaurant, decorated with driftwood and

wildlife prints, has a stunning view of Florida Bay and serves reasonably priced meals. The daily breakfast buffet is a bargain at $5.25 per person, with a carafe of coffee included. Cereal, Danish, fresh fruit, granola, muffins, and cinnamon-honey butter are offered daily, along with a tasty array of hot items. The kitchen also will prepare box lunches and serves a full dinner menu. Fishermen should not pass up the opportunity to have the chef prepare their day's catch for $7.75 per person, including all the trimmings. Mango cheesecake and mud pie are among the desserts.

The park has three campgrounds — at Flamingo, Long Pine Key, and Chekika State Recreation Area. **Flamingo** offers almost 300 campsites, each with a picnic bench and charcoal grill. Recreational vehicles are allowed, but there are no electrical or water hookups. A fee of $8.00 per night is charged for sites you can drive to and $4.00 per night for walk-up sites. I prefer the latter. The walk isn't very far, and some of the sites are directly on Florida Bay.

Veteran campers tell me that the cold showers at Flamingo are not unusually frigid, but I suspect those folks must be members of local Polar Bear Clubs back home. The bugs are abominable in the summer — camping is free then for anyone brave enough to try it — but tolerable in the winter if you use repellent.

Raccoons are a big concern, especially if you camp at a drive-up site next to the mangroves. Do not bring food or water into your tent unless you're prepared to entertain some four-legged visitors. Raccoons can unzip zippers, including those on your tent. Foraging raccoons brushed against the side of my tent one night and climbed atop the raised grill another evening to sift through the briquettes. They look cute but can carry rabies. Feeding them is against the law.

Buzzards, or vultures, also can be a nuisance, particularly around walk-up sites. They perch on top of rest rooms and wait for unwary campers to leave containers of food and trash bags unattended. In a matter of minutes, scraps are spread all over the ground.

Despite these drawbacks, the campground at Flamingo is full or close to it through most of the winter. It is convenient to prime bird-watching areas and the marina, site of a number of boat tours, tram rides, and bicycle, canoe, and skiff rentals.

Most ranger programs originate at the Flamingo Visitor Center, where activity schedules and park information is available. A small museum is located adjacent to the visitors center.

The wildlife in the Flamingo area also makes it an attractive destination. Alligators and crocodiles can be seen around the marina, bald eagles sometime perch atop channel markers in Florida Bay, and birds by the hundreds gather at Eco Pond, only a few minutes' walk from the campground. Unusual wildlife sightings are posted in the visitors center.

Film, gasoline, groceries, and ice can be purchased at the marina store, which also stocks camping and fishing supplies.

Fishing for redfish, snook, and trout in the waters surrounding Flamingo can be tremendous, with many captured as close to the marina as Joe Kemp Key, accessible by canoe or skiff. (Rentals are available at the marina.) Be sure to check on license requirements and what is in season.

Fishing from shore is more difficult but can be productive. Small tarpon are caught at night near the fish-cleaning table on the Whitewater Bay side of the marina, and sheepheads and trout are taken from the shore behind the campground.

Interdenominational worship services are conducted at Flamingo twice a day on Sunday during the winter season. The schedule is posted outside the restaurant.

Long Pine Key, six miles past the main entrance, is convenient to the Royal Palm Visitor Center and is the most attractive of the campgrounds. Its 108 sites surround a lake, and each site has a picnic bench, charcoal grill, and surfaced parking pad.

The cost is $8.00 per night. The only drawback is that there are no showers.

Chekika State Recreation Area, which is north of Homestead and west of Krome Avenue, is a popular summer site. It has a spring-fed artesian pond and nice freshwater beach, and the lake is good for fishing. Each of its twenty sites is equipped with a picnic table and grill, and there are hot and cold showers. The cost is $8.00 per night.

The campgrounds at Long Pine Key and Chekika were closed during the winter of 1993 due to problems caused by Hurricane Andrew. They are both expected to reopen in the fall of 1993.

All three of the campgrounds are wonderful for stargazing on clear, crisp winter nights. Make sure you come equipped for cool – and sometimes even cold – weather. Temperatures are usually comfortable during the day and in the fifties or sixties at night, but temperatures occasionally dip into the forties or below.

A palate-pleasing stop en route to the main park entrance is the Robert is Here fruit stand in Homestead. You will be tempted by exotic tropical fruits such as carambolas, coconuts, mameys, and sapodillas, as well as traditional tropical offerings such as grapefruits, oranges, tangelos, and tangerines. Employees will slice your purchase into bite-size pieces so that you can eat and browse at the same time.

The shelves also are stocked with homemade jellies, marmalades, and preserves. Jellies include guava, hot Vidalia onion, key lime, passion fruit, red pepper, spicy tomato, and sea grape. Kumquat, orange, and tangerine-lime are among the marmalades, and litchi, mango, and papaya are on the list of preserves.

No trip is complete without sampling one of Robert's blended-to-order fruit shakes. My favorite is the mango-tango.

The stand, which survived the full force of Hurricane Andrew with amazingly little damage, is a ten-minute drive from the main entrance to Everglades National Park on State 9336, the road that leads to the park from US 1 in Homestead.

Hurricane Andrew devastated motels and hotels in the surrounding area. About half of the two dozen or so in the vicinity had not yet reopened seven months after the storm. Several had to be razed. A list of accommodations, restaurants, pick-your-own fields, and other attractions is available from the Tropical Everglades Visitor Center, which is on the west side of US 1 in Homestead, just south of Burger King.

WEST LAKE

Crocodiles had been seen crossing the Snake Bight Trail and swimming in the Buttonwood Canal, but I went to West Lake to learn about them and their environment. A fickle female crocodile looking for a place to lay eggs had park officials in an uproar a few years ago. First she made a nest in front of the West Lake Visitor Center, prompting maintenance workers to rope off the area. Then she created another nest a short distance away, so close to the road that her snout rested on the pavement when she tried to lay her eggs. Finally, she dug in a spot on the roadside and laid thirty-two eggs beside the sign at West Lake. Thirteen hatched and were dispersed in the area around the lake.

Endangered due to loss of habitat, crocodiles are believed to number only about 500 in South Florida. A small number live in Everglades National Park and frequent West Lake because of its high salt content and surrounding mangrove forest.

Crocodiles are far more reclusive than alligators, so you probably won't see any here. But hearing about them is enjoyable, and so is exploring the junglelike environment they prefer.

Ranger-guided tours are scheduled regularly at West Lake, located seven miles from Flamingo. Programs consist of a fifteen-minute lecture on alligators and crocodiles and then a one-hour walk on a quarter-mile boardwalk through a mangrove forest.

Mangroves are the lifeblood of South Florida's marine ecosystem. The federally protected trees provide a nursery for birds, crabs, fish, lobsters, marine mammals, and shrimp, and the dense, nearly impenetrable thickets help to mitigate storm damage. Hurricane Andrew destroyed approximately 70,000 acres of mangroves in South Florida, but none of that damage occurred at West Lake. Here trees still bear scars from 1960's Hurricane Donna, which leveled mangroves sixty to eighty feet tall with 180 mph gusts.

Mangroves still tower twenty to twenty-five feet above both sides of the boardwalk, which begins and ends at the parking area and juts a short distance into West Lake, a brackish estuary where the natural freshwater flow of the Everglades mixes with salt water from the Gulf of Mexico. Three types of mangroves — red, black, and white — grow here, as well as buttonwood and strangler figs.

Red mangroves have thick, waxy, dark green leaves and a root system that looks like a spider's legs. Black mangroves have smooth, dark bark and leaves that are green on top and light gray on the bottom. White mangroves have yellowish green leaves and glands at the base of the leaf through which they excrete salt. The leaves of the white mangrove were used as a source of salt in pioneer cooking. The wood of the black mangrove was burned to repel mosquitoes at the turn of the century.

The black mangrove estuary is the lone breeding ground for salt-marsh mosquitoes, which makes this area an unpleasant place to visit during the summer rainy season. Alligators, crocodiles, raccoons, river otters, snakes, and wood rats are among the inhabitants of the mangrove community, along with game fish such as snook, which forage for food around mangrove roots. One member of our tour group also found a tiny hair ball that had apparently been spit out by an owl. That and some tiny bones were all that remained of the unlucky mouse.

Young herons' vertical pose makes them hard to see among the trees

SWAMP TROMP

We met on the roadside a few miles north of Paurotis Pond. Ranger Christi Carmichael briefed us on our mission – to get the feel of the Everglades – and then handed out walking sticks fashioned from broom handles. We would have been sunk – literally – without them.

Few activities are as useful as a Swamp Tromp for introducing visitors to the park's unique environment. In a matter of seconds, you go from the relative comfort of dry land to messy, mushy marl.

Eight of us followed Carmichael single-file as she waded into the marsh. "The initial step is always the worst," she warned.

A few audible gasps were emitted as we sank past our ankles in periphyton, the spongy algae carpet that rests beneath the river of grass. One woman, wearing hip boots and waders, fell when one of her feet slipped into a crack in the limestone floor, where water remains in times of drought.

"Don't be embarrassed," Carmichael said. "I have people on their backs, faces, and butts all the time."

One middle-aged woman fell to her knees and decided to turn back. The rest of us pressed on.

Carmichael ambled forward as unencumbered as a wading bird. We struggled good-naturedly behind her. At one point, my boat shoes got sucked off.

"Walking is harder than it looks," Carmichael quipped. "It's almost like walking through the tundra."

An hour of determined tromping brought us to a hardwood hammock – an elevated stand of tropical trees. We had covered a whole half mile in an hour.

"It's amazing how much energy it takes to get here," Carmichael noted. "It's really not that far."

The effort is worth it, though. Around us were dwarf

cypress trees that could have been one hundred years old. We could see poisonwood trees, saw palmettos, wax myrtles, and paurotis palms, which have a slender trunk and fan-shaped leaves.

The ranger pointed out dense underbrush where bobcats and endangered panthers sometimes sleep. "It's hard for me to imagine that a panther uses this type of an environment as a hunting ground, but they do," Carmichael said. "A lot of animals find a way to get in."

Carmichael picked up an aquatic apple snail for all to see. The creature is the lone food source for the endangered snail kite, whose population dipped to twenty to twenty-five birds in North America in the early 1960s because of the prolonged drought.

Forty-five minutes later, we returned to the road, a bit more quickly than when we had begun, but plodding nonetheless. Carmichael invited us back, with or without her. "Visitors are invited to do this on their own anytime," she said. "But you have to look out for snakes as you enter the water."

CANOE TOURS

Rangers lead free two- to four-hour canoe tours several times a week on Florida Bay or any of a half dozen designated trails set aside exclusively for canoes. Trips are posted several days in advance at the Flamingo Visitor Center, and participants are usually chosen via lottery. Visitors are allowed to take only one guided canoe trip a season to ensure that others get a chance.

Canoes also can be rented from concessionaires at the Flamingo marina and West Lake, thirty-one miles past the park's main entrance. Fees range from $7.00 per hour to $25.00 per day, and canoes can be transported to other areas.

Canoeing is best out of Flamingo during low tide, when

thousands of birds rest on nearby sandbars. More protected areas are better on windy days. When the air is still, mosquitoes can be a problem even with heavy-duty repellent, especially in the summer.

The Everglades offers the following canoe trails:

• Nine Mile Pond. A 5.2-mile loop takes you through a shallow saw grass marsh with scattered mangrove islands.

• Noble Hammock. This 2-mile trail winds through a maze of shady mangrove-lined creeks and small ponds. Sharp corners and narrow passageways require good maneuverability, but this is a calm trail even on a windy day. Check for low water levels during the dry season.

• Hells Bay. This sheltered route weaves through mangrove creeks and ponds to a series of small bays. The trail – hell to get into and out of – is marked with 160 numbered poles. Distances vary depending on your destination but can be as far as 11 miles round-trip.

• Florida Bay. Watch birds at Snake Bight during medium to low tide, fish, or just enjoy the scenery.

• Bear Lake Canal. Many tropical plants and trees are visible along this narrow, tree-covered trail, which is 1.6 miles to Bear Lake and 11.5 miles one way to Cape Sable. It is impassable between markers 13 and 17 during the dry winter season.

• Mud Lake Loop. This 6.8-mile loop connects the Buttonwood Canal, Coot Bay, Mud Lake, and the Bear Lake Canoe Trail. Birding is often good at Mud Lake. Boats with motors are prohibited on Mud Lake, Bear Lake, and the Bear Lake Canal.

• West Lake. This trail leads 7.7 miles to Alligator Creek, passing through a series of large, open lakes connected by narrow creeks lined with mangroves. This is alligator and crocodile territory and not recommended on windy days due to exposed, rough water.

PADDLING ON NINE MILE POND

A dozen of us, two to a canoe, paddled across Nine Mile Pond and headed for the River of Grass. It was a glorious winter morning — perfect for canoeing in the Everglades — with bright blue skies, a slight breeze, and temperatures in the sixties.

Immediately, we recognized how lucky we were to be in the company of Christi Carmichael, a park ranger who has led countless tours on this scenic 5.2-mile trail through a saw grass marsh. Although the route is well marked, it is still possible to get confused as you become preoccupied with the fascinating scenery. Carmichael told us that a ranger got lost here years ago and had to be led out by a helicopter. Instinctively, we all paddled a bit faster and followed her as closely as we could.

Carmichael lead us through narrow passages between red mangroves, saltwater trees whose seeds were deposited in this freshwater estuary by the wind. We paddled past hammocks, slightly elevated islands where tropical hardwoods grow and mammals such as bobcats and panthers hide during the day. We continued on through saw grass, a long, thin grass with a saw-toothed edge; spike rush; and bladderwort, a carnivorous plant with yellow flowers that trap unsuspecting insects.

We stroked briskly past impassive alligators, barely visible in the water except for their snouts. A nervous twelve-inch baby gator, unseen when perched atop a mangroves sinewy roots, plopped into the water as we approached.

A nine-inch green anole climbed higher into the mangroves and bobbed its head in defiance when we came a little too close. These native lizards throw out a red throat pouch for mating and territorial purposes and have toes that spread out like a parachute when they jump.

Our paddling interrupted bluegills and largemouth bass fanning beds for reproduction and stirred up the bottom to reveal occasional apple snails — the only food for the endangered snail kite. Ospreys and red-shouldered hawks circled overhead, cormorants dove for fish, and an unseen palm warbler called to us from the trees.

Carmichael called back, but the bird didn't show itself. Neither did three bald eagles that nested here the previous year. We returned to where we had put in our canoes by paddling through a series of ponds not visible from the road.

BIRD-WATCHING TOURS

We had been walking the half-mile trail at Eco Pond for only a few minutes when ranger Becky Zurcher hushed us to a stop. A smooth-billed ani was perched in the midst of many great southern white butterflies a few feet away. The significance of this escaped those of us who are beginner bird-watchers.

Zurcher told us that birders come here specifically to see this species, but the anis rarely show themselves. She said that her husband had worked at the park for three straight winters and had never seen one.

The bird, which resembles a grackle with a down-turned beak and a rounded, elongated tail, seemed oblivious to us. It dined on a butterfly as we watched.

Then our focus was diverted by a bald eagle circling overhead. When we returned our attention to the ani, the elusive bird was gone.

You needn't be an ardent birder to identify rare and beautiful birds in Everglades National Park. There are so many, especially in the winter, that all you need to do is look.

Beginners, or those with only casual interest, benefit greatly from the free, regularly scheduled bird-watching tours. The one that I joined originated at Eco Pond, an eight-acre lake within walking distance of the Flamingo campground, and continued to Mrazek and Nine Mile ponds. The latter two, both popular bird-watching venues, are five- and eleven-mile drives from Flamingo.

Our group met at the observation deck at Eco Pond, a shallow, man-made wetland that receives purified water from the Flamingo sewage treatment plant. We watched a belted kingfisher dive repeatedly at the surface of the water, then return to the same perch every time. Then we saw an anhinga plunge into the water, stab a fish with its bill, toss it in the air, and swallow it headfirst. A white ibis stuck its long, down-turned bill into the mud to search for crawfish and crabs as a green-backed heron flew overhead. In trees across the pond, we could see a black-crowned night heron, a roseate spoonbill, and a pink ibis at roost.

We would have stayed on the platform all day if Zurcher hadn't reminded us we had much more to see. She led us on a short walk around one side of the pond, where we saw, in addition to the ani, an alligator, a blue crab, an eagle, a tricolored heron, tropical buckeye butterflies, and zebra butterflies. We missed the scissortail flycatchers and flocks of cedar waxwings other casual birders had seen on a similar tour, but we weren't disappointed.

From there, we drove to Mrazek Pond, the most popular bird-watching site in the park. Cameras clicked and whirred as photographers zeroed in on an endangered wood stork perched across the pond. Wood storks, whose breeding cycle is upset when the natural flow of waterways is diverted, may no longer nest in South Florida by the year 2000.

Photographers also focused on a great egret, which stood on a branch hanging over the water and occasionally slapped the surface with a stick it held in its mouth. "It's fishing," the ranger said. "Sometimes they even catch insects and drop them on top of the water to trick a fish into coming up to check it out."

Next we adjourned to Nine Mile Pond, where we saw double-crested cormorants, a great blue heron, a belted kingfisher, an osprey, and a swallow-tailed kite. Ospreys and eagles vie for food here. Ospreys catch fish in death-defying dives from fifty feet above the water, only to lose them when wily eagles bully them away. The two predators scream and fight over ownership in midair, but the eagle usually wins.

BIG CYPRESS NATIONAL PRESERVE

Artist Sam Vinikoff has been painting Everglades landscapes for more than three decades. It is here, in the Big Cypress Swamp, that he sets up an easel and does his best work. I felt incredibly lucky to bump into Vinikoff one March morning at the visitors center and jumped at the invitation to follow him around. Few people know the preserve's 2,400 square miles better than he.

Big Cypress National Preserve, created by Congress in 1974, is vastly different from adjacent Everglades National Park. Although plants and animals are generally protected, certain activities prohibited in most national parks are tolerated in the preserve. Among these are the hunting and trapping of game animals, oil and gas exploration, and cattle grazing. As distasteful as some of these uses might seem, the impact is less noticeable than, say, logging in Ocala National Forest. The one exception is that game animals are far more skittish here than in the Everglades, for obvious reasons.

The best way to see Big Cypress, other than by walking a portion of the Florida National Scenic Trail, is by car. Hundreds of endangered wood storks were roosting in trees along the canal on US 41 five miles east of the visitors center when I toured the area in the spring of 1993. Numerous alligators and wading birds were sharing the opposite bank, and gars and largemouth bass were swimming in the canal.

Safer and more scenic sightseeing can be done from the much less busy Turner River Road (County 839) and Loop Road (State 94). I chose the former first because that's Vinikoff's favorite place. He drove a van with a graceful American swallow-tailed kite painted on its side and pulled over several times to point out interesting sights. Eventually, he pulled over to paint, and I continued down the unpaved road, leaving swirling clouds of dust behind me.

Great egrets and ibis were too numerous to count. Anhingas and cormorants perched atop limbs extending out over the river, and turtles sunned themselves on logs. A river otter crossed the road ahead of me, and when I stopped to watch it, I found myself staring at half a dozen brightly colored baby alligators trying to hide in the thick vegetation along the shore.

A great egret

An hour later, as I returned to where Vinikoff was already nearly done with a canvas, two white-tailed deer bolted across the road thirty yards away. If I had arrived fifteen seconds earlier, the animals would still have been swimming across the river, and I would have had little difficulty photographing them. In the time it took me to cover the thirty yards, the deer had gone five times that distance through rough terrain, tails bouncing in the air.

I lunched with the artist and accompanied him down an unnamed, unmarked trail that crosses a levee over the river. We looked for deer tracks and woodpecker nests in the cavities of cabbage palms and hoped to see wood storks rise from the wet grass. We didn't, but the companionship and shared love of nature made the experience special.

On a return trip a few days later, I drove along the fascinating Loop Road, a mostly unimproved road that I wouldn't recommend to anyone with a recreational vehicle. The swamp through which Loop Road passes is wild and untamed. Dwarf cypress trees grow at the edge of the road, with water reaching a few feet up the trunks. In some places, the canopy of trees completely covers the road up ahead. The road is so narrow that one car has to pull over to let another pass.

Wood storks roosted on one side of the road, and great blue herons and great egrets waded unconcerned. I stopped and took a few casts in fishy-looking areas. I caught several big bluegills and spotted tilapias on a small-surface lure called a Rapala. Both species are good to eat, but I released them.

A number of hunting camps and the shacks of squatters are visible from the road. I wouldn't suggest stopping to visit, however, because this is a place where people come to lose themselves in nature. The few residents are feisty and suspicious of intruders.

Camping is permitted in a number of campgrounds that are either directly on US 41 or only a short distance away. The exception is the campground at Bear Island, an hour's drive inland on Turner River Road. (County 839). All facilities are primitive and lack water, rest rooms, benches, and grills. Those who prefer more basic amenities will find them in one commercial campground on US 41 or can stay in a bed and breakfast or motel in Everglades City, about forty-five minutes away.

Bringing food and water is essential on any trip into Big Cypress National Preserve. Sunscreen and insect repellent are important, too.

Where: Twenty-four hundred square miles north and west of Everglades National Park in south-central and southwest Florida. The easiest route of entry is US 41, which connects Miami with Naples.

Hours: The Big Cypress Preserve Visitor Center, formerly called the Oasis Visitor Center, is open from 8:30 A.M. to 4:30 P.M. daily except Christmas. It is fifty miles west of Miami and fifty-five miles southeast of Naples on US 41.

Admission: None.

Best time to visit: Highest visitation is in January and February, when the weather is mild and bird activity has begun. It is also busy during hunting season, which runs from September through December.

Concessions: None.

Activities: No guided programs are offered. Bird watching, camping, fishing, hiking, hunting, and off-road vehicle use are the most popular recreations.

Pets: Allowed in the preserve's campgrounds but not recommended due to the abundance of alligators and other wild animals.

Other: A fifteen-minute orientation film is offered at the visitors center, where field guides and other literature are sold and maps are distributed. The smallest active post office in the United States is along US 41 in Ochopee.

For more information:

Big Cypress National Preserve, HCR 61 P.O. Box 110, Ochopee, FL 33943. 813-695-4111 or 813-262-1066.

FAKAHATCHEE STRAND STATE PRESERVE

The 75,000-acre Fakahatchee Strand State Preserve is managed as a natural area and has extremely limited recreational facilities, but don't let that deter you. Its pine flatwoods, cypress and hardwood swamps, wet prairies, marshes, mangroves, bays, and creeks warrant investigation.

The area's dense, vegetated swamps are called strands because they tend to be long and narrow. Fakahatchee Strand, twenty miles long and three to five miles wide, is the largest in the region of the Big Cypress Swamp.

The flow of water through the strand is essential to its health and that of the estuaries south of it, and its natural value may be greater than that of any area of comparable size in the state. The strand sustains a remarkable diversity of plant and animal life, much of it unique to this part of the world. The cypress strands here and at Audubon's Corkscrew Swamp Sanctuary (see page 106) are the last places you can still see large numbers of the giant trees. Several large stands of royal palms also are scattered throughout the swamp, which has the largest concentrations of these trees in the world.

Exploring this area isn't easy, but you shouldn't neglect it for that reason. It offers a scenic drive and boardwalk, as well as plenty of opportunities to strike out on your own. All, for the most part, can be done in one full day.

Fakahatchee Strand has no designated trails, but people do some hiking on their own, usually using old logging roads to access the swamp. Hikers should contact preserve headquarters before setting out and should be prepared to tackle a challenging environment that includes waist-deep water, cypress knees, submerged logs, biting insects, and reptiles. Alligators and water snakes abound, although they are wary of humans and are not a problem as long as you use common sense. Because the swamp is dense, hikers should be adept at using a topographic map and compass to find their way out. Such items must be purchased elsewhere, as there are no specialty stores closer than Naples.

Three- to four-hour swamp walks are offered monthly from November through April beginning at preserve headquarters, just west of the tiny settlement of Copeland. Groups are limited to fifteen and are almost always full, so reservations are a must. Participants wade directly into the swamp, making long pants and lace-up boots necessary. Make sure to bring plenty of bottled water and a lunch.

Many of the excursions end up at remote lakes that serve as feeding pools for animals, anhingas, kingfishers, and wading birds. Scenery en route to and around the shallow lakes is lush and varied, with pond apple trees covered by orchids, bromeliads, ferns, and royal palms. Epiphytes — plants that grow on trees high off the ground and get their nutrients from the air and rain – are so plentiful that hikers find themselves peering up at branches rather than down at the ground.

For those who want to get a feel for Fakahatchee Strand without getting their feet wet, the preserve offers a free, 2,000-foot boardwalk at Big Cypress Bend on US 41 and a twelve-mile, one-way drive on W.J. Janes Memorial Scenic Drive. The latter starts at Copeland and ends at the park boundary at South Golden Gate Estates, a rural community where Florida black bears, a threatened species, are causing concern by wandering into people's backyards. The drive goes through several wetland habitats, including a prairie, a royal palm hammock, and a cypress forest.

Alligators, bears, bobcats, deer, raccoons, river otters, snakes, and turtles are occasionally seen at Fakahatchee Strand. The small, dwindling population of endangered panthers traverses the preserve and several other state and federal lands in southwest Florida, but don't expect to see one. The animals are reclusive and regularly range over an area of 175 square miles.

Other endangered and threatened species that call Fakahatchee Strand home include the eastern brown pelican, Everglades mink, Florida sandhill crane, Mangrove fox squirrel, peregrine falcon, red-cockaded woodpecker, southern bald eagle, and West Indian manatee.

I chose to take the W. J. Janes Memorial Scenic Drive in the morning and returned to walk on the boardwalk in the late afternoon. The drive, on a narrow gravel road, begins just past the preserve headquarters and takes anywhere from 90 minutes to 2.5 hours depending on how often you stop and explore.

A few minutes into the drive, I happened upon a turtle sitting in the middle of the road. I got out and took a picture from ten feet away without the turtle's becoming the least bit concerned. Not long after that, I interrupted a black racer as it started to cross the road. The snake slithered quickly back into the grass as soon as my car approached.

Three different times, I stopped to watch raccoons through binoculars as they foraged along the roadside one hundred yards ahead of me. Another time, I stopped to stretch my legs and was startled to discover a twelve-foot alligator sunning itself across a pool ten yards from me.

A buck with a healthy rack of antlers ran in front of my car about one hundred yards after I made the turnaround at the boundary of the preserve. I slammed on my brakes and watched it disappear, only to have a doe dash across the road twenty-five yards away.

The only disconcerting moment came when I observed a fellow target shooting at Florida gars with a .22-caliber rifle from the bank at the bridge that marks the end of the preserve. Even the gar – a species loathed by sportfishermen but loved by alligators – are protected within the preserve. I reported the violation to the first ranger I saw.

The walk around the boardwalk, located seven miles north of the intersection of US 41 and State 29, was even more pleasing. The boardwalk extends into Fakahatchee Strand's Big Cypress Bend region, an area designated a national natural landmark because of the many virgin cypress trees that still remain. This part of the strand looks much as it did when the first Europeans arrived in America.

In some places along the boardwalk, cypress trees are as big as eighty to one hundred feet tall and more than twenty feet around. In some cases, the roots of strangler figs climb fifty to sixty feet up the trees, most of which have bromeliads growing on branches and in crevices in their trunks.

The deeper into the swamp you go, the more breathtaking it becomes. The boardwalk ends at an observation area, where you can look out over a pond shrouded by huge trees. Gars slapped at the surface, and a half dozen baby alligators nine to twelve inches long milled about. A cottonmouth was curled up at the base of a tree three feet from the walk.

Where: The Big Cypress Bend boardwalk is on US 41 approximately 7 miles north of the intersection of State 29 and US 41. The W. J. Janes Memorial Scenic Drive (County 837 West) is off State 29, 2.5 miles north of US 41.

Hours: The boardwalk is open from 8:00 A.M. to sundown daily. The drive is best in the early morning or late afternoon when wildlife is most active.

Admission: Free.

Best time to visit: November through April.

Activities: Strenuous swamp walks through cypress swamps and pond apple sloughs are held once a month from November through April. Reservations are necessary.

Concessions: None.

Pets: Not allowed. Guide dogs are always welcome.

Other: Literature is available at the ranger station in Copeland. Pack a lunch and bring drinks since there is nothing available.

For more information:

Fakahatchee Strand State Preserve, P.O. Box 548, Copeland, FL 33926. 813-695-4593.

SHARK VALLEY

Everglades National Park, established in 1947, was the first national park created for biological rather than aesthetic reasons. A visit to Shark Valley, about an hour's drive southwest of downtown Miami, shows why.

The Everglades are in danger of dying of thirst. The clean, natural flow of water necessary for their survival has been diverted and suppressed by a management system designed to meet the needs prompted by runaway development. Water that once streamed seventy miles south into the Everglades from Lake Okeechobee must now negotiate an obstacle course that includes a 400,000-acre agricultural area and 1,400 canals, dams, and other containment structures.

"It's like cutting off your head and expecting your legs to keep walking," park ranger Steve Collins said. "It just doesn't work."

Nutrients, pesticides, and pollutants introduced into the ecosystem through farm fields have stimulated the growth of nonnative plants such as cattails, which are taking over saw grass prairies at a rate of four acres per day. Animals and fish are being poisoned by mercury leaching into the environment from unknown sources, prompting warnings to limit the consumption of freshwater fish.

"We have done a lot to upset the balance of nature," Collins said. "People are just beginning to learn how this ecosystem works and what makes it healthy. More than anything else, what this park needs is a voice. It needs people to speak up for the alligators, the birds, and the trees."

A two-hour, ranger-guided tram tour in Shark Valley is well worth your time. Trips leave every hour between 9:00 A.M. and 4:00 P.M. and are a bargain at $7.30 for adults and $3.65 for kids. "It is so beautiful, no one would ever believe you," a first-time visitor riding aboard my tram said.

The tram carries visitors the fifteen-mile length of the Shark Valley Loop Road through saw grass prairies, hammocks, bay heads, and willow heads. It stops for twenty minutes at a sixty-five foot observation tower that opens up on stunning vistas.

The day I visited, a half dozen alligators were sunbathing on a canal bank beneath the observation tower, two turtles swam slowly in the crystal-clear water below, and anhingas, cormorants, great blue herons, and white ibis roosted in adjacent trees. Virginia white-tailed deer, which eat the celerylike shoots of saw grass, ambled through the marsh half a mile away.

The tram crept within inches of alligators up to nine feet

long during the course of the tour, and we saw literally dozens of others along the side of the road. We also crossed paths with great blue herons, four-foot wading birds with wingspans wider than our tram, and saw plenty of anhingas, cormorants, great white herons, little blue herons, little green herons, pied-billed grebes, terns, turkey vultures, and white ibis as well.

Steve Collins, our tour guide, got out of the tram and stepped into the marsh at one point to retrieve periphyton, the spongy algae that carpets the Everglades. The ranger passed out pieces for us to examine before returning it to the swamp.

The tram also stopped so Collins could point out a hardwood hammock, bay head, and willow head, all thriving within a few hundred yards of the road. As many as 200 species of plants and trees grow in hardwood hammocks, slightly elevated islands in the saw grass. Bay heads (bay tree islands that rest on mucky ground) provide habitat for insects and food for birds, lizards, and snakes. Willow heads form in slight depressions and retain water during droughts, like watering holes in African savannas.

Alligators help clear the willow heads of muck and sticks and make them more hospitable for other creatures. "He creates his own little McDonald's because sooner or later everything has to come there," Collins said.

We saw a doe and a fawn nibbling roots half a mile from the Shark Valley Visitor Center as our tram ride neared its completion. We also saw an eight-foot alligator resting beside the road with its jaws agape – the reptile's equivalent of panting.

"You will be amazed at what this place has to offer," Collins noted. "It is one of the few places where the slower you move, the more there is to see. If you stick your nose into places you see a lot, even if you are just walking around. You don't have to go very far."

Two easily negotiable walking trails are located within half a mile of the visitors center. Special activities, including

NOTES

The only "people food" available in Shark Valley is soda and snacks sold from vending machines. You can get a full meal at the Miccosukee Restaurant, which is across from the entrance to Shark Valley on US 41. Skip standard fare in favor of Miccosukee fry bread ($1.75) or pumpkin bread ($1.85), both served hot with butter. The bread is almost a meal in itself. The menu also includes frog legs ($12.25), catfish ($12.25), and hush puppies ($1.85).

The Miccosukee Tribe of Florida, recognized by the U.S. government in 1962, maintains an information center next to the restaurant and a culture center and village half a mile farther west on US 41. An admission fee of $5.00 for adults and $3.50 for children ages four to twelve is charged. Native crafts, short airboat tours ($7.00 per half hour), and alligator-wrestling shows are offered. A number of other commercial airboat tours are available along US 41, none of which is allowed to enter Everglades National Park.

Accommodations are extremely limited in the vicinity of Shark Valley. One small motel, the Everglades Tower, is located a few miles west on US 41. In the winter, rooms are $59.00.

Campsites are available in the Big Cypress National Preserve, at distances ranging from nine to eighty-three miles from Shark Valley. Ask for a list of campsites at the entrance station to Shark Valley. Camping is free but without amenities such as picnic benches, grills, and water.

The campground where I stayed at 50-Mile Bend surrounds a small lake brimming with fish. Although amenities are nonexistent, the atmosphere is pleasant at night, with people sitting around fires and talking, singing, or playing the harmonica. Stargazing is wonderful.

Fishing is not allowed in Shark Valley but can be good for bluegills, catfish, and largemouth bass in the canal on the north side of US 41. A state freshwater fishing license – $13.50 annually for residents and $16.50 for seven days for nonresidents – is necessary. Licenses and bait can be purchased at Dade Corners and Ned's Bait and Tackle, eighteen and thirteen miles east of Shark Valley on US 41.

Most fish caught should be released, as health warnings have been posted because of possible mercury contamination. Pregnant women should not eat any fish. Other adults should limit consumption to one fish per month.

early-morning wildlife tram tours and sunset and full-moon tours, are scheduled in the winter.

Many people rent bicycles (for $2.13 per hour) to explore the Shark Valley Loop Road at their leisure. Bicyclists are requested to travel opposite the flow of tram traffic and are required to pull off to the side when a tram approaches. The entire fifteen-mile trip takes an average of two to three hours. Regulations require groups of more than two bicyclists and after-hours bicycle groups to obtain a special-use permit. Applications are available at the visitors center.

Where: Thirty miles west of Miami off US 41.
Hours: 8:30 A.M. to 6:00 P.M. daily year-round.
Admission: $4.00 per vehicle, $2.00 for bicyclists, bus passengers, and pedestrians.
Best time to visit: Winter.
Activities: Tram rides, bicycle tours, talks, and walks.
Concessions: Bicycles can be rented for $2.13 per hour. Two-hour tram tours are $7.30 for adults and $3.65 for children. Tours begin every hour on the hour from 9:00 A.M. to 4:00 P.M.
Pets: None are allowed.
Other: Film, literature, and park maps are available at the visitors center from 8:30 A.M. to 5:15 P.M. daily.
For more information:
Everglades National Park, P.O. Box 279, Homestead, FL 33030. 305-221-8776. Please send a self-addressed, stamped envelope.

EVERGLADES NATIONAL PARK GULF COAST RANGER STATION

Captain Joe Chapman pointed his double-deck tour boat at a mangrove island in Chokoloskee Bay and then brought it to a sudden stop. A peregrine falcon, perched halfway up a tree, had almost escaped unnoticed.

The bird, twenty feet off the bow, blended in so well with its surroundings that it was nearly indiscernible. But Chapman kept maneuvering his vessel until all seventy-five passengers had caught a glimpse of the largest falcon seen in Florida. The sightings of the falcon, one of the most spectacular birds of prey, was the highlight of a thrilling 2.5-hour trip taken out of the Gulf Coast Ranger Station.

Ranger-narrated boat tours are the best way to see this popular visitors area, the entry point for exploring the mangrove islands and estuaries of the Ten Thousand Islands. Short trips are offered almost hourly throughout the day, but I recommend the lengthier excursion to Kingston Key. It includes a thirty-minute stroll on a deserted beach at the edge of the Gulf of Mexico and is truly a bargain at $13.78.

The tour began with a close look at a colony of black skimmers, a long-winged ternlike bird that skims the surface as it feeds on fish and shrimp. Within a few minutes of leaving the dock, we also saw our first osprey, considered a threatened species in Florida due to habitat loss and environmental contaminants. The osprey, roosting in a tall snag atop a mangrove island, was one of only a few not to have had most its nest blown away during a freak winter storm that struck the eastern United States on March 13, 1993.

The tour took us past islands formed over thousands of years atop mounds of oyster shells discarded by Calusa and Seminole Indians. We navigated around mangrove islands, passing canoeists and kayakers along the way.

A school of bottle-nosed dolphins swam in our wake. A flock of brown pelicans skimmed the surface in one direction; a group of royal terns sat on a sandbar in another. The beach walk, amid cacti, horseshoe crabs, sea oats, and shells, also was a treat.

We returned from Kingston Key by a different route, which gave us a look at some new scenery. A double-crested cormorant, a diving bird that is used by fishermen to retrieve fish in the Orient, rested on a stump on the point of a mangrove island. A great blue heron was difficult to see as it stood among mangrove roots. A great egret, a snowy egret, a white ibis, and a little blue heron perched on branches overhanging the water.

Passengers on our boat's upper deck had an opportunity to look down into a massive osprey nest as we rode within a few yards of a channel marker. The mother and two chicks were in the nest on top of the marker. All of us watched in wonder as black-crowned night herons flew overhead.

In the last half hour, we saw both the peregrine falcon and an endangered manatee. The falcon stared coldly at us as we jockeyed close enough for everyone to see. The West Indian manatee, a walruslike mammal that feeds on aquatic plants, poked its nostrils through the surface briefly before returning to the bottom of Chokoloskee Bay, where it grazes on sea grass the same way a cow does in a pasture.

Where: Everglades City, eighty miles west of Miami and forty miles southeast of Naples via US 41 and County 29.
Hours: The visitors center is open from 7:30 A.M. to 5:00 P.M. during the busy winter season and has shorter hours, generally 9:00 A.M. to 5:00 P.M., in the summer.
Admission: None.
Best time to visit: Winter and spring.
Activities: Naturalist-narrated beach walks and boat trips, canoe tours, and talks. Backcountry canoe camping is allowed for free with a permit obtained at the ranger station. This is the starting point for the one hundred-mile Wilderness Waterway, a marked trail for canoeists from Everglades City to Flamingo, with primitive campsites along the way.
Concessions: Boat tours leave the marina adjacent to the ranger station about every half hour between 9:00 A.M. and 5:00 P.M. during the winter and once every hour in the summer. The cost

is $10.60 for a one-hour tour and $13.78 for a 2.5-hour trip. Seventeen-foot canoes can be rented at the ranger station for $20.00 per day or $15.00 per half day. Canoes also can be rented from North American Canoe Tours in Everglades City (813-695-4666) for $20.00 per day or $16.00 per half day. A small cooler of ice and a quart of water are included. North American also provides canoes and camping equipment for extended backcountry stays for $50.00 per person per day for the first day and $45.00 per person for each additional day. Cost includes a tent, cooking equipment, a battery-operated lantern, water jugs, and one cooler. Men's and women's bikes, three-wheelers, and bicycles-built-for-two can be rented from Ride My Bike in Everglades City (813-695-2111). Bikes also are available from the Ivey House bed and breakfast in Everglades City from November 1 through March 31 for $1.00 per hour for guests and $3.00 per hour for nonguests.

Pets: Allowed on a leash in a small picnic area outside the ranger station. They are not permitted in the backcountry.

Other: Gifts and snacks are available on the lower level on the ranger station from 8:30 A.M. to 5:00 P.M. Park-related literature and other environmental books are sold at the Everglades City Welcome Center at the intersection of US 41 and County 29. Bait, books, camping supplies, charts, food, and maps can be purchased across from the ranger station at the Glades Haven Recreational Resort (813-695-2746) from 6:00 A.M. to 9:00 P.M. daily.

For more information:

Everglades National Park Gulf Coast Ranger Station, P.O. Box 120, Everglades City, FL 33939. 813-695-3311.

Index

Titles in the Green Guide series:

Fall 1993
Green Guide to Hawaii
Green Guide to Oregon
Green Guide to Washington

Spring 1994
Green Guide to Alaska
Green Guide to Idaho
Green Guide to Maine
Green Guide to New Hampshire
Green Guide to New Jersey
Green Guide to Ohio

Fall 1994
Green Guide to Massachusetts
Green Guide to Northern California
Green Guide to Southern California
Green Guide to Texas
Green Guide to Virginia

All books are $9.95 at bookstores.
Or order directly from the publisher (add $3.00 shipping and handling for direct orders):

Country Roads Press
P.O. Box 286
Castine, Maine 04421
Toll-free phone number: **800-729-9179**